DEDICATION

To Laila, Sarah, and Peter

CONTENTS

ACKNOWLEDGMENTS

I am extremely grateful to Katy, who plowed through my piles of obscure books and beyond to check it; to Sarah, whose design so enhanced it; to Monica, whose splendid work kept things together; and to the special, encouraging friends (you know who you are) who have made this all possible.

Above all, I am profoundly grateful to the authors and editors who have produced superb work on this issue for so many years, many receiving little personal gain despite the excellence and dedication of their labors.

I am eternally indebted to the *Washington Report on Middle East Affairs*, which has covered this issue for thirty years, and its superb book club, an unparalleled resource. I am similarly deeply thankful to *The Link* and its 40 years of brilliant, in-depth journalism on the Middle East, all on a shoestring budget.

I could not have written this book without the superlative work of previous writers and researchers in revealing the facts on the history of the US-Israeli relationship. I have had the profound honor of meeting some of the top authors on this topic in person and cannot thank them enough for their ground-breaking work: Alfred Lilienthal, Richard Curtiss, Stephen Green, Kathleen Christison, and, especially, Donald Neff, whose detailed research and exquisite writing first opened my eyes to the real history of US-Israel relations.

I find it extremely sad that these extraordinary publications and authors are not more celebrated. If their work had been more widely known and the facts they exposed had reached more of the American electorate, I feel it is quite possible that some of today's deeply erroneous policies might have been avoided – and that numerous individuals now dead might be living. My hope to change this situation has motivated my own small contribution. Any mistakes in the following volume are, of course, my own.

PREFACE

I hadn't originally meant to write a book.

For over a dozen years I had been reading excellent books containing facts about the history of US-Israel relations that very few people seemed to know – even individuals highly knowledgeable about the history of the Middle East.

Because so few people are aware of this information, inaccurate narratives have frequently dominated discussions of the US-Israel relationship, contributing to highly flawed U.S. policies. Such policies have fueled tragedy in the region and damage to Americans.

I finally decided to write an article that would set the record straight.

My article, however, grew longer and longer, as I realized how much there was to explain. Plus, I continued to find more information that I felt people needed to know. I would research a point to confirm the information I had, and would often stumble across additional facts of significance, often ones that were extremely surprising to me. The article became a book.

There are two somewhat unusual aspects to this book.

First, I have placed almost as much information in my endnotes section as in the main body of the book.

This is largely because, given how busy most people are, my goal was to write a short, succinct book on the basics. I especially wanted the book to be useful to readers new to this issue, who I felt would be best served by a concise, clear sketch of what has been going on.

At the same time, however, there were additional details that I thought would be interesting to many people, even if this information did not merit being included in the main account. Therefore, I decided to include it in the endnotes.

I felt these additional facts would be particularly valuable to people who have studied this issue for years and yet who probably had not come across much of this information. I also felt this additional information would be interesting to neophytes after they had read an overall account of the basic history.

Another reason for the lengthiness of the endnotes section is that during my research I occasionally came across information that contained speculative hypotheses that I thought merited investigation. This information, too, I placed in the endnotes, suggesting that other researchers might wish to explore it further.

A second unusual aspect of this book is that beginning several years ago I published my early, rough drafts as I went along – both on the Internet and in print booklets.

This was because fairly early on in my writing I realized that this project was going to take far longer than I had originally anticipated. Since I felt it was critical that the facts get out to people as soon as possible, I decided to make my information available to others quickly, rather than waiting for a finished manuscript. I also posted some critical documents ahead of time, so that others, also, could read them. Happily, I suspect this practice has caused other books, published since I began making my research public, to address aspects that might otherwise have been omitted.

* * *

I am often asked how and why I became so intensely interested in Israel-Palestine.

This was certainly unexpected; earlier in my life I would not have predicted that I would write a book on this topic. Like most Americans I felt this region had little to do with me. I had never paid much attention to this issue, and my information about it was largely influenced by the movie Exodus and mainstream U.S. news headlines.

In the fall of 2000 that changed.

What is now known as the "Second Intifada" (Palestinian uprising) was in the news, and I grew curious about it. I decided to follow the news coverage to learn what this conflict was all about, and I fairly quickly noticed how one-sided the coverage was. My background was in journalism (I was at that time the editor of a very small weekly community newspaper), so I was aware that reporters are supposed to give the full picture in a more complete way than I felt was going on.

Because the Internet was available, making information on remote daily events far more accessible than previously, I began to research the news further. In doing so I discovered a far more drastic pattern of Israeli violence against Palestinians than mainstream U.S. news organizations were revealing.

For example, I discovered that large numbers of Palestinian children were being killed by Israeli forces, many of them through gunfire to the head – and that they had been killed before the far smaller number of Israeli children who eventually began also to be tragically killed. Similarly, I found that over 140 Palestinians of all ages had been killed before any Israelis in Israel, even though the media consistently were referring to Israeli violence as retaliatory.

After a few months of looking into this issue, becoming more and more disturbed by what I was finding in the region – and what began to appear to me to be a cover-up in the American media – I finally decided I needed to see for myself what was going on. I quit my job and went to the region as a freelance reporter, traveling independently throughout Gaza and the West Bank during the height of the uprising.

When I returned, I began an organization called "If Americans Knew." The purpose was to create a nonpartisan, journalistic organization that would provide the facts on this extremely important issue to the American public, and on our connection to it.

Americans have given far more of our tax money to Israel than to any other nation, and to the region in general. In addition, the U.S. government frequently vetoes international initiatives on Israel that virtually all other nations endorse. As a result, our support for Israel has created growing hostility against the United States, placing our citizens in increasing risk.*

I began to read voraciously on the subject. I was particularly curious about the history of the conflict, and of how the United States became so involved, since I felt that to understand a current situation, it is essential to understand what created it.

In the course of my reading, I discovered a great many startling facts and a history of my own nation of which I had been almost entirely unaware. I suspect that others will share my considerable surprise.

After nearly a decade and a half of researching this issue, including a number of trips to the region, I have come to view the U.S. connection to Israel as one of the most critical issues in the world today, and one of the most urgent for Americans to understand.

The lack of engagement by people such as myself fourteen years ago has allowed fanatics to drive U.S. policies. I feel it is essential, both for other nations and for our own, that the rest of us become involved.

I have now begun work on a second small volume, which will take the history of US-Israel relations through to the present. Please stay tuned.

– Alison Weir
Sacramento, California
February, 2014

* A collection of my articles from my trip and since will be published in the coming year. These contain citations for the above facts.

Chapter One

HOW THE U.S. "SPECIAL RELATIONSHIP" WITH ISRAEL CAME ABOUT

While many people are led to believe that U.S. support for Israel is driven by the American establishment and U.S. national interests, the facts don't support this theory. The reality is that for decades U.S. foreign policy and defense experts opposed supporting the creation of Israel. They then similarly opposed the massive American funding and diplomatic support that sustained the forcibly established state and that provided a blank check for its aggressive expansion. They were simply outmaneuvered and eventually replaced.

Like many American policies, U.S. Middle East policies are driven by a special interest lobby. However, the Israel Lobby, as it is called today in the U.S.[1], consists of vastly more than what most people envision in the word "lobby."

As this book will demonstrate, the Israel Lobby is considerably more powerful and pervasive than other lobbies. Components of it, both individuals and groups, have worked underground, secretly and even illegally throughout its history, as documented by scholars and participants.

And even though the movement for Israel has been operating in the U.S. for over a hundred years, most Americans are completely unaware of this movement and its attendant ideology – a measure of its unique influence over public knowledge.

The success of this movement to achieve its goals, partly due to the hidden nature of much of its activity, has been staggering. It has also come at an almost unimaginable cost.

It has led to massive tragedy in the Middle East: a hundred-year war of violence and loss; sacred land soaked in sorrow.

In addition, this movement has been profoundly damaging to the United States itself.

As we will see in this two-part examination of the pro-Israel movement, it has targeted virtually every significant sector of American society; worked to involve Americans in tragic, unnecessary, and profoundly costly wars; dominated Congress for decades; increasingly determined which candidates could become serious contenders for the U.S. presidency; and promoted bigotry toward an entire population, religion and culture.

It has promoted policies that have exposed Americans to growing danger, and then exaggerated this danger (while disguising its cause), fueling actions that dismember some of our nation's most fundamental freedoms and cherished principles.[2]

All this for a population that is considerably smaller than New Jersey's.[3]

Chapter Two

THE BEGINNINGS

The Israel Lobby in the U.S. is just the tip of an older and far larger iceberg known as "political Zionism," an international movement that began in the late 1800s with the goal of creating a Jewish state somewhere in the world. In 1897 this movement, led by a European journalist named Theodor Herzl[4], coalesced in the First Zionist Congress, held in Basel, Switzerland, which established the World Zionist Organization, representing 117 groups the first year; 900 the next.[5]

While Zionists considered such places as Argentina, Uganda, the Mediterranean island of Cyprus, and Texas,[6] they eventually settled on Palestine for the location of their proposed Jewish State, even though Palestine was already inhabited by a population that was 93-96 percent non-Jewish. The best analysis says the population was 96 percent Muslims and Christians,[7] who owned 99 percent of the land.[8]

After the Zionist Congress, Vienna's rabbis sent two of their number to explore Palestine as a possible Jewish state. These rabbis recognized the obstacle that Palestinians presented to the plan, writing home: "The bride is beautiful, but she is married to another man."[9] Still, Zionists ultimately pushed forward. Numerous Zionist diary entries, letters, and other documents show that they decided to push out these non-Jews – financially, if possible; violently if necessary.[10]

Political Zionism in the U.S.

The importance of the United States to this movement was recognized from early on. One of the founders of political Zionism, Max Nordau, wrote a few years after the Basel conference, "Zionism's only hope is the Jews of America."[11]

At that time, and for decades after, the large majority of Jewish Americans were not Zionists. In fact, many actively opposed Zionism. In the coming years, however, Zionists were to woo them assiduously with every means at hand. The extent to which Nordau's hope was eventually realized is indicated by the statement by a prominent author on Jewish history, Naomi Cohen, who in 2003 wrote, "but for the financial support and political pressure of American Jews... Israel might not have been born in 1948."[12] To this might be added Zionists' success in influencing American politicians, the media, and much of the general public.

Groups advocating the setting up of a Jewish state had first begun popping up around the United States in the 1880s.[13] Emma Lazarus, the poet whose words would adorn the Statue of Liberty, promoted Zionism throughout this decade.[14] A precursor to the Israeli flag was created in Boston in 1891.[15]

In 1887 President Grover Cleveland appointed a Jewish ambassador to Turkey (seat of the Ottoman Empire, which at that time controlled Palestine), because of Palestine's importance to Zionists. Jewish historian David G. Dalin reports that presidents considered the Turkish embassy important to "the growing number of Zionists within the American Jewish electorate."[16]

Every president, both Republican and Democrat, followed this precedent for the next 30 years. "During this era, the ambassadorship to Turkey came to be considered a quasi-Jewish domain," writes Dalin. [17]

By the early 1890s organizations promoting Zionism existed in New York, Chicago, Baltimore, Milwaukee, Boston, Philadelphia, and Cleveland.[18]

Reports from the Zionist World Congress in Basel, which four Americans had attended, gave this movement a major stimulus, galvanizing Zionist activities in American cities that had large Jewish populations.[19]

In 1897-98 Zionists founded numerous additional societies throughout the East and the Midwest. In 1898 they converged in a first annual conference of American Zionists, held in New York on July 4th. There they formed the Federation of American Zionists (FAZ).[20]

By the 1910s the number of Zionists in the U.S. approached 20,000 and included lawyers, professors, and businessmen. Even in its infancy, when it was still relatively weak, and represented only a tiny fraction of the American Jewish population, Zionism was becoming a movement to which "Congressmen, particularly in the eastern cities, began to listen."[21]

The movement continued to expand. By 1914 several additional Zionist groups had formed, including Hadassah, the women's Zionist organization.[22] By 1918 there were 200,000 Zionists in the U.S., and by 1948 this had grown to almost a million. [23]

From early on Zionists actively pushed their agenda in the media. One Zionist organizer proudly proclaimed in 1912 "the zealous and incessant propaganda which is carried on by countless societies." The Yiddish press from a very early period espoused the Zionist cause. By 1923 every New York Yiddish newspaper except one was Zionist. Yiddish dailies reached 535,000 families in 1927.[24]

While Zionists were making major inroads in influencing Congress and the media, State Department officials were less enamored with Zionists, who they felt were trying to use the American government for a project damaging to the United States. Unlike politicians, State Department officials were not dependent on votes and campaign donations. They were charged with recommending and implementing policies beneficial to all Americans, not just one tiny sliver working on behalf of a foreign entity. [25]

In memo after memo, year after year, U.S. diplomatic and military experts pointed out that Zionism was counter to both U.S. interests and principles.

While more examples will be discussed later, Secretary of State Philander Knox was perhaps the first in the pattern of State Department officials rejecting Zionist advances. In 1912, the Zionist Literary Society approached the Taft administration for an endorsement. Knox turned them down flat, noting that "problems of Zionism involve certain matters primarily related to the interests of countries other than our own."[26]

Despite that small setback in 1912, Zionists garnered a far more significant victory in the same year, one that was to have enormous consequences both internationally and in the United States and that was part of a pattern of influence that continues through today.

Chapter Three

LOUIS BRANDEIS, ZIONISM, AND THE "PARUSHIM"

In 1912 prominent Jewish American attorney Louis Brandeis, who was to go on to become a Supreme Court Justice, became a Zionist.[27] Within two years he became head of the international Zionist Central Office, newly moved to America from Germany.[28]

While Brandeis is an unusually well known Supreme Court Justice, most Americans are unaware of the significant role he played in World War I and of his connection to Palestine.

Some of this work was done with Felix Frankfurter, who became a Supreme Court Justice two decades later.

Perhaps the aspect of Brandeis that is least known to the general public – and often even to academics – is the extent of his zealotry and the degree to which he used covert methods to achieve his aims.

While today Brandeis is held in extremely high esteem by almost all Americans, there was significant opposition at the time to his appointment to the Supreme Court, largely centered on widespread accusations of unethical behavior. A typical example was the view that Brandeis was "a man who has certain high ideals in his imagination, but who is utterly unscrupulous, in method in reaching them."[29]

While today such criticisms of Brandeis are either ignored or attributed to political differences and/or "anti-Semitism,"[30] there is evidence suggesting that such views may have been more accurate than Brandeis partisans would like.

In 1982 historian Bruce Allen Murphy, in a book that won a Certificate of Merit from the American Bar Association, reported that Brandeis and Frankfurter had secretly collaborated over many years on numerous covert political activities. Zionism was one of them.[31]

"[I]n one of the most unique arrangements in the Court's history, Brandeis enlisted Frankfurter, then a professor at Harvard Law School, as his paid political lobbyist and lieutenant," writes Murphy, in his book *The Brandeis/Frankfurter Connection: The Secret Political Activities of Two Supreme Court Justices.* "Working together over a period of 25 years, they placed a network of disciples in positions of influence, and labored diligently for the enactment of their desired programs."[32]

"This adroit use of the politically skillful Frankfurter as an intermediary enabled Brandeis to keep his considerable political endeavors hidden from the public," continues Murphy.[33]

Brandeis only mentioned the arrangement to one other person, Murphy writes, "another Zionist lieutenant– Court of Appeals Judge Julian Mack."[34]

One reason Brandeis and Frankfurter kept their arrangement secret was that such behavior by a sitting Supreme Court justice is considered highly unethical. As an editorial in the *New York Times* pointed out following the publication of Murphy's book, "... the Brandeis-Frankfurter arrangement was wrong. It serves neither history nor ethics to judge it more kindly, as some seem disposed to do... the prolonged, meddlesome Brandeis-Frankfurter arrangement violates ethical standards."

The *Times* reiterates a point also made by Murphy: the fact that Brandeis and Frankfurter kept their arrangement secret demonstrated that they knew it was unethical – or at least realized that the public would view it as such: "They were dodging the public's appropriate measure of fitness."[35]

Later, when Frankfurter himself became a Supreme Court Justice, he used similar methods, "placing his own network of disciples in various agencies and working through this network for the realization of his own goals." These included both Zionist objectives and "Frankfurter's stewardship of FDR's programs to bring the U.S. into battle against Hitler."[36]

Their activities, Murphy notes, were "part of a vast, carefully planned and orchestrated political crusade undertaken first by Brandeis through Frankfurter and then by Frankfurter on his own to accomplish extrajudicial political goals."[37]

Frankfurter had joined the Harvard faculty in 1914 at the age of 31, a post gained after a Brandeis-initiated donation from financier Jacob Schiff to Harvard created a position for Frankfurter.[38] Then, Murphy writes, "for the next 25 years, [Frankfurter] shaped the minds of generations of the nation's most elite law students."[39]

After Brandeis become head of the American Zionist movement, he "created an advisory council–an inner circle of his closest advisers–and appointed Felix Frankfurter as one of its members."[40]

The Parushim

Even more surprising to this author – and even less well-known both to the public and to academics – is Brandeis's membership in a secret society that covertly pushed Zionism both in the U.S. and internationally.[41]

Israeli professor Dr. Sarah Schmidt first reported this information in an article about the society published in 1978 in the *American Jewish Historical* Quarterly. She also devoted a chapter to the society in a 1995 book. Author and former *New York Times* editor Peter Grose, sympathetic to Zionism,[42] also reported on it in both a book and several subsequent articles. [43]

According to Grose, a highly regarded author, Brandeis was a leader of "an elitist secret society called the Parushim, the Hebrew word for 'Pharisees' and 'separate,' which grew out of Harvard's Menorah Society."[44]

Schmidt writes: "The image that emerges of the Parushim is that of a secret underground guerilla force determined to influence the course of events in a quiet, anonymous way."

Grose writes that Brandeis used the Parushim "as a private intellectual cadre, a pool of manpower for various assignments."[45] Brandeis recruited ambitious young men, often from Harvard, to work on the Zionist cause – and further their careers in the process.

"As the Harvard men spread out across the land in their professional pursuits," Grose reports, "their interests in Zionism were kept alive by secretive exchanges and the trappings of a fraternal order. Each invited initiate underwent a solemn ceremony, swearing the oath 'to guard and to obey and to keep secret the laws and the labor of the fellowship, its existence and its aims.'"[46]

At the secret initiation ceremony, new members were told:

> "You are about to take a step which will bind you to a single cause for all your life. You will for one year be subject to an absolute duty whose call you will be impelled to heed at any time, in any place, and at any cost. And ever after, until our purpose shall be accomplished, you will be fellow of a brotherhood whose bond you will regard as greater than any other in your life–dearer than that of family, of school, of nation."[47]

While Brandeis was a key leader of the Parushim, an academic named Horace M. Kallen was its founder, creating it in 1913. Kallen was an academic first hired by Woodrow Wilson, who was then president of Princeton, to teach English there.[48] When Kallen founded the Parushim he was a philosophy professor at the University of Wisconsin in Madison. Kallen is generally considered the father of cultural pluralism.

In her book on Kallen, Schmidt includes more information on the society in a chapter entitled, "Kallen's Secret Army: The Parushim."

She reports, "A member swearing allegiance to the Parushim felt something of the spirit of commitment to a secret military fellowship." [49]

"Kallen invited no one to become a member until the candidate had given specific assurances regarding devotion and resolution to the Zionist cause," Schmidt writes, "and each initiate had to undergo a rigorous analysis of his qualifications, loyalty, and willingness to take orders from the Order's Executive Council."[50] Not surprisingly, it appears that Frankfurter was a member.[51]

'We must work silently, through education and infection'

Members of the Parushim were quite clear about the necessity of keeping their activities secret. An early recruiter to the Parushim explained: "An organization which has the aims we have must be anonymous, must work silently,[52] and through education and infection rather than through force and noise." He wrote that to work openly would be "suicidal" for their objective.[53]

Grose describes how the group worked toward achieving its goals: "The members set about meeting people of influence here and there, casually, on a friendly basis. They planted suggestions for action to further the Zionist cause long before official government planners had come up with anything."

"For example," Grose writes, "as early as November 1915, a leader of the Parushim went around suggesting that the British might gain some benefit from a formal declaration in support of a Jewish national homeland in Palestine."[54] (More on this in the following chapter.)

Brandeis was a close friend of President Woodrow Wilson and used this access to advocate for the Zionist cause, at times serving as a conduit between British Zionists and the president.[55]

In 1916 President Wilson named Brandeis to the Supreme Court. At that time, as was required by standard ethics, Brandeis gave in to pressure to officially resign from all his private clubs and affiliations, including his leadership of Zionism. But behind the scenes he continued this Zionist work, quietly receiving daily reports in his Supreme Court chambers and issuing orders to his loyal lieutenants.[56]

When the Zionist Organization of America (ZOA) was reorganized in 1918, Brandeis was listed as its "honorary president." However, he was more than just "honorary."

As historian Donald Neff writes, "Through his lieutenants, he remained the power behind the throne." One of these lieutenants, of course, was Frankfurter. [57]

Zionist membership expanded dramatically during World War I, despite the efforts of some Jewish anti-Zionists, one of whom called the movement a "foreign, un-American, racist, and separatist phenomenon."[58]

Chapter Four

World War I & the Balfour Declaration

Most analysts consider WWI a pointless conflict that resulted from diplomatic entanglements rather than some travesty of justice or aggression. Yet, it was catastrophic to a generation of Europeans, killing 14 million people.[59]

The United States joined this unnecessary war a few years into the hostilities, costing many American lives, even though the U.S. was not party to the alliances that had drawn other nations into the fray. This even though Americans had been strongly opposed to entering the war and Woodrow Wilson had won the presidency with the slogan, "He kept us out of war."[60]

President Wilson changed course in 1917 and plunged the U.S. into that tragic European conflict. Approximately 270,000 Americans were killed or injured.[61] Over 1,200 American citizens who opposed the war were rounded up and imprisoned, some for years.[62]

A number or reasons were publicly given for Wilson's change of heart, including Germany's submarine warfare, Germany's sinking of the American passenger ship

Lusitania, and a diplomatic debacle known as the Zimmerman Telegram episode.[63] Historians also add pro-British propaganda and economic reasons to the list of causes, and most suggest that a number of factors were at play.

While Americans today are aware of many of these facts, few know that Zionism appears to have been one of those factors.

Diverse documentary evidence shows that Zionists pushed for the U.S. to enter the war on Britain's side as part of a deal to gain British support for their colonization of Palestine.

From the very beginning of their movement, Zionists realized that if they were to succeed in their goal of creating a Jewish state on land that was already inhabited by non-Jews, they needed backing from one of the "great powers."[64] They tried the Ottoman Empire, which controlled Palestine at the time, but were turned down (although they were told that Jews could settle throughout other parts of the Ottoman empire and become Turkish citizens).[65]

They then turned to Britain, which was also initially less than enthusiastic. Famous English Middle East experts such as Gertrude Bell pointed out that Palestine was Arab and that Jerusalem was sacred to all three major monotheistic faiths.[66]

Future British Foreign Minister Lord George Curzon similarly stated that Palestine was already inhabited by half a million Arabs who would "not be content either to be expropriated for Jewish immigrants or to act merely as hewers of wood and drawers of water for the latter."[67]

However, once the British were embroiled in World War I, and particularly during 1916, a disastrous year for the Allies in which there were 60,000 British casualties in one day alone,[68] Zionists were able to play a winning card. While they previously had appealed to religious or idealistic arguments, now Zionist leaders could add a particularly powerful motivator: telling the British government that Zionists in the U.S. would push America to enter the war on the side of the British, if the British promised to support a Jewish home in Palestine afterward.[69]

In 1917 British Foreign Minister Lord Balfour issued a letter to Zionist leader Lord Rothschild. Known as the Balfour Declaration, this letter promised that Britain would "view with favour the establishment in Palestine of a national home for the Jewish people" and "use their best endeavours to facilitate the achievement of this object."

The letter then qualified this somewhat by stating that it should be "clearly understood that nothing shall be done which may prejudice the civil and religious rights of existing non-Jewish communities in Palestine." The "non-Jewish communities" were 92 percent of Palestine's population at that time,[70] vigorous Zionist immigration efforts having slightly expanded the percentage of Jews living in Palestine by then.

The letter, while officially signed by British Foreign Minister Lord Balfour, had been in process for two years and had gone through a number of edits by British and American Zionists and British officials.[71] As Zionist leader Nahum Sokolow later wrote, "[e]very idea born in London was tested by the Zionist Organization in America, and every suggestion in America received the most careful attention in London."[72]

Sokolow wrote that British Zionists were helped, "above all, by American Zionists. Between London, New York, and Washington there was constant communication, either by telegraph, or by personal visit, and as a result there was perfect unity among the Zionists of both hemispheres." Sokolow particularly praised "the beneficent personal influence of the Honourable Louis D. Brandeis, Judge of the Supreme Court."[73]

The final version of the Declaration was actually written by Leopold Amery, a British official who, it came out later, was a secret and fervent Zionist.[74]

It appears that the idea for such a declaration had been originally promoted by Parushim founder Horace Kallen.

Author Peter Grose reports, "The idea had come to [the British] from an unlikely source. In November 1915, long before the United States was involved in the war, the fertile brain of Horace Kallen... had come up with the idea of an Allied statement supporting in whatever veiled way was deemed necessary, Jewish national rights in Palestine."

Grose writes that Kallen suggested the idea to a well-connected British friend who would pass the idea along. According to Kallen, such a statement "would give a natural outlet for the spontaneous pro-English, French, and Italian sympathies of the Jewish masses." Kallen told his friend that this would help break down America's neutrality, which Kallen knew was the aim of British diplomacy, desperate to bring the U.S. into the war on its side.

Grose writes: "Kallen's idea lit a spark of interest in Whitehall."[75]

While the "Balfour Declaration" was a less than ringing endorsement of Zionism, Zionists considered it a major breakthrough, because it cracked open a door that they would later force wider and wider open. In fact, many credit this as a key factor in the creation of Israel.[76]

These Balfour-WWI negotiations are referred to in various documents.

Samuel Landman, secretary of the World Zionist Organization, described them in detail in a 1936 article in *World Jewry*. He explained that a secret "gentleman's agreement" had been made in 1916 between the British government and Zionist leaders:

> "After an understanding had been arrived at between Sir Mark Sykes and [Zionists] Weizmann and Sokolow, it was resolved to send a secret message to Justice Brandeis that the British Cabinet would help the Jews to gain Palestine in return for active Jewish sympathy and for support in the USA for the Allied cause, so as to bring about a radical pro-Ally tendency in the United States."[77]

Landman wrote that once the British had agreed to help the Zionists, this information was communicated to the press, which he reported rapidly began to favor the U.S. joining the war on the side of Britain.[78]

Landman claimed that Zionists had fulfilled their side of the contract and that it was "Jewish help that brought U.S.A. into the war on the side of the Allies," thus causing the defeat of Germany.[79] He went on to state that this had "rankled" in Germany ever since and "contributed in no small measure to the prominence which anti-Semitism occupies in the Nazi programme."

British Colonial Secretary Lord Cavendish also wrote about this agreement and its result in a 1923 memorandum to the British Cabinet, stating: "The object [of the Balfour Declaration] was to enlist the sympathies on the Allied side of influential Jews and Jewish organizations all over the world... [and] it is arguable that the negotiations with the Zionists...did in fact have considerable effect in advancing the date at which the United States government intervened in the war."[80]

Former British Prime Minister Lloyd George similarly referred to the deal, telling a British commission in 1935: "Zionist leaders gave us a definite promise that, if the Allies committed themselves to giving facilities for the establishment of a national home for the Jews in Palestine, they would do their best to rally Jewish sentiment and support throughout the world to the Allied cause. They kept their word."[81]

Brandeis University professor and author Frank E. Manuel reported that Lloyd George had testified in 1937 "that stimulating the war effort of American Jews was one of the major motives which, during a harrowing period in the European war, actuated members of the cabinet in finally casting their votes for the Declaration."[82]

American career Foreign Service Officer Evan M. Wilson, who had served as Minister-Consul General in Jerusalem, also described this arrangement in his book *Decision on Palestine*. He wrote that the Balfour declaration "...was given to the Jews largely for the purpose of enlisting Jewish support in the war and of forestalling a similar promise by the Central Powers [Britain's enemies in World War I]".[83]

The official biographer of Lloyd George, author Malcolm Thomson, stated that the "determining factor" in the decision to issue the Balfour Declaration was the "scheme for engaging by some such concession the support of American Zionists for the allied cause in the first world war."[84]

Similarly, Zionist historian Naomi Cohen calls the Balfour Declaration a "wartime measure," and writes: "Its immediate object was to capture Jewish sympathy, especially in the United States, for the Allies and to shore up England's strategic interests in the Near East." The Declaration was pushed, she writes, "by leading Zionists in England and by Brandeis, who intervened with President Wilson."[85]

Finally, David Ben-Gurion, the first prime minister of Israel, wrote in 1939: "To a certain extent America had played a decisive role in the First World War, and American Jewry had a considerable part, knowingly or not, in the achievement of the Balfour Declaration."[86]

The influence of Brandeis and other Zionists in the U.S. had enabled Zionists to form an alliance with Britain, one of the world's great powers, a remarkable achievement for a non-state group and a measure of Zionists' by-then immense power. As historian Kolsky states, the Zionist movement was now "an important force in international politics."[87]

American Zionists may also have played a role in preventing an early peace with the Ottoman Empire.[88]

In May 1917 American Secretary of State Robert Lansing received a report that the Ottomans were extremely weary of the war and that it might be possible to induce them to break with Germany and make a separate peace with Britain.[89]

Such a peace would have helped in Britain's effort to win the war (victory was still far from ensured), but it would have prevented Britain from acquiring Palestine and enabling a Jewish state.[90]

The State Department considered a separate Ottoman peace a long shot, but decided to send an emissary to pursue the possibility. Felix Frankfurter became part of the delegation and ultimately persuaded the delegation's leader, former Ambassador Henry J. Morgenthau, to abandon the effort.[91]

US State Department officials considered that Zionists had worked to scuttle this potentially peace-making mission and were unhappy about it.[92] Zionists often construed such displeasure at their actions as evidence of American diplomats' "anti-Semitism."

Chapter Five

PARIS PEACE CONFERENCE 1919: ZIONISTS DEFEAT CALLS FOR SELF-DETERMINATION

After the war, the victors met in a peace conference and agreed to a set of peace accords that addressed, among many issues, the fate of the Ottoman Empire's Middle East territories. The Allies stripped the defeated Empire of its Middle Eastern holdings and divided them between Britain and France, which were to hold them under a "mandate" system until the populations were "ready" for self-government. Britain got the mandate over Palestine.

Zionists, including Brandeis, Felix Frankfurter, World Zionist Organization officials, and an American delegation, went to the peace conference to lobby for a Jewish "home"[93] in Palestine and to push for Balfour wording to be incorporated in the peace accords. The official U.S. delegation to the peace conference also contained a number of highly placed Zionists.

Distinguished American Christians posted in the Middle East, who consistently supported Arab self-determination, went to Paris to oppose Zionists. Numerous prominent Christian leaders in the U.S. – including two of the most celebrated pastors of their day, Harry Emerson Fosdick and Henry Sloane Coffin – also opposed Zionism.[94] However, as a pro-Israel author notes, they were "simply outgunned" by Zionists.[95]

The most influential American in the Middle East at the time, Dr. Howard Bliss, President of Beirut's Syrian Protestant College (later to become the American University of Beirut), traveled to Paris to urge forming a commission to determine what the people of the Middle East wanted for themselves, a suggestion that was embraced by the U.S. diplomatic staff in Paris.[96]

Princeton Professor Philip Brown, in Cairo for the YMCA, supplied requested reports to the U.S. State Department on what Zionism's impact would be on Palestine. He stated that it would be disastrous for both Arabs and Jews and went to Paris to lobby against it.[97]

William Westermann, director of the State Department's Western Asia Division, which covered the region, similarly opposed the Zionist position. He wrote that "[it] impinges upon the rights and the desires of most of the Arab population of Palestine." Westermann and other U.S. diplomats felt that the Arab position was much more in line with Wilson's principles of self-determination and circulated Arab material.[98]

President Wilson decided to send a commission to Palestine to investigate the situation in person. After spending two months in the area interviewing all sections of the population, the commission, known as the King-

Crane commission, recommended against the Zionist position of unlimited immigration of Jews to make Palestine a distinctly Jewish state.[99]

The commissioners stated that the creation of a Jewish state in Palestine could be accomplished only with "the gravest trespass upon the civil and religious rights of existing non-Jewish communities in Palestine," pointing out that to subject the Palestinians "to steady financial and social pressure to surrender the land, would be a gross violation of the principle [of self-determination] and of the peoples' rights…"[100]

They went on to point out that "the well-being and development" of the people in the region formed "a sacred trust," that the people should become completely free, and that the national governments "should derive their authority from the initiative and free choice of the native populations."[101]

The report stated that meetings with Jewish representatives made it clear that "the Zionists looked forward to a practically complete dispossession of the present non-Jewish inhabitants of Palestine," concluded that armed force would be required to accomplish this, and urged the Peace Conference to dismiss the Zionist proposals.[102] The commission recommended that "the project for making Palestine distinctly a Jewish commonwealth should be given up."[103]

Zionists through Brandeis dominated the situation, however, and the report was suppressed until after the Peace Accords were enacted.[104] As a pro-Israel historian noted, "with the burial of the King-Crane Report, a major obstacle in the Zionist path disappeared."[105] The U.S. delegation was forced to follow Zionist directives.[106]

Ultimately, the mandate over Palestine given to Britain supported the Zionist project and included the Balfour language. According to the mandate, Britain would be "responsible for putting into effect the [Balfour] declaration ... in favor of the establishment in Palestine of a national home for the Jewish people, it being clearly understood that nothing should be done which might prejudice the civil and religious rights of existing non-Jewish communities in Palestine...."[107]

Chapter Six

FORGING AN "INGATHERING" OF ALL JEWS

The idea behind Zionism was to create a state where Jews worldwide could escape anti-Semitism.[108] Combined with this was the belief that all Jews would and should come to the Jewish state in a massive "ingathering of exiles."[109] However, when it turned out that not enough Jews were coming of their own volition, a variety of methods were used to increase the immigration. Zionist leader David Ben-Gurion once told a gathering of Jewish Americans: "[Zionism] consists of bringing all Jews to Israel. We appeal to the parents to help us bring their children here. Even if they decline to help, we will bring the youth to Israel; but I hope that this will not be necessary."[110]

There are various documented cases in which fanatical Zionists exploited, exaggerated, invented, or even perpetrated "anti-Semitic" incidents both to procure support and to drive Jews to immigrate to the Zionist-designated homeland. A few examples are discussed below.

Brandeis and Frankfurter vs. U.S. diplomat

One such case involved a young diplomat named Hugh Gibson, who in 1919 was nominated to be U.S. Ambassador to Poland. After he arrived in Poland, Gibson, who was highly regarded and considered particularly brilliant,[111] began to report that there were far fewer anti-Semitic incidents than Americans were led to believe. He wrote his mother: "These yarns are exclusively of foreign manufacture for anti-Polish purposes."[112]

His dispatches came to the attention of Brandeis and his protégé (and future Supreme Court Justice) Felix Frankfurter, who demanded a meeting with Gibson. Gibson later wrote of their accusations:

> "I had [Brandeis and Frankfurter claimed] done more mischief to the Jewish race than anyone who had lived in the last century. They said…that my reports on the Jewish question had gone around the world and had undone their work…. They finally said that I had stated that the stories of excesses against the Jews were exaggerated, to which I replied that they certainly were and I should think any Jew would be glad to know it."[113]

Frankfurter hinted that if Gibson continued these reports, Zionists would block his confirmation by the Senate.

Gibson was outraged and sent a 21-page letter to the State Department. In it he shared his suspicions that this was part of "a conscienceless and cold-blooded plan to make the condition of the Jews in Poland so bad that they must turn to Zionism for relief."

Zionists and Nazis

Perhaps the most extreme case of Zionist exploitation of anti-Semitism to further their cause came during the rise of Adolf Hitler.

Zionist leaders had a mixed response to Hitler and the rise of the Nazis. Israeli historian Tom Segev writes, "Everyone wondered how the persecution of the Jews in Germany would affect life in Palestine." While papers predicted "loss and ruin beyond repair" and described a "dance of death" in Berlin, "they expected that 'the hour of trouble and anguish' would open unprecedented historical opportunities–specifically, increased immigration to Palestine. Ben-Gurion hoped the Nazis' victory would become 'a fertile force' for Zionism."[114]

Historians have documented that Zionists sabotaged efforts to find safe havens for Jewish refugees from Nazi Germany in order to convince the world that Jews could only be safe in a Jewish state.[115]

When FDR made efforts in 1938[116] and 1943[117], and the British in 1947[118], to provide havens for refugees from the Nazis, Zionists opposed these projects because they did not include Palestine.

Morris Ernst, FDR's international envoy for refugees, wrote in his memoir that when he worked to help find refuge for those fleeing Hitler, "...active Jewish leaders decried, sneered and then attacked me as if I were a traitor. At one dinner party I was openly accused of furthering this plan of freer immigration [into the U.S.] in order to undermine political Zionism… Zionist friends of mine opposed it."[119]

Ernst wrote that he found the same fanatical reaction among all the Jewish groups he approached, whose leaders, he found, were "little concerned about human blood if it is not their own."[120]

FDR finally gave up, telling Ernst: "We can't put it over because the dominant vocal Jewish leadership of America won't stand for it."[121]

Journalist Erskine B. Childers, son of a former Irish Prime Minister, wrote in the *Spectator* in 1960, "One of the most massively important features of the entire Palestine struggle was that Zionism deliberately arranged that the plight of the wretched survivors of Hitlerism should be a 'moral argument' which the West had to accept."

He explained that "this was done by seeing to it that Western countries did not open their doors, widely and immediately, to the inmate of the DP [displaced persons] camps."

Childers, author of several books on conflict resolution and peace-keeping who later became Secretary General of the World Federation of United Nations Associations, commented: "It is incredible that so grave and grim a campaign has received so little attention in accounts of the Palestine struggle – it was a campaign that literally shaped all subsequent history. It was done by sabotaging specific Western schemes to admit Jewish DPs."[122]

There was even a certain amount of collusion between Zionists and Nazi leaders. When disturbing facts emerged in the 1950s about this, these caused considerable scandal in Israel and led to the fall of the Israeli government of the time. A number of books are dedicated to this subject and it is discussed in numerous others. In some cases there were accusations that Zionist collaboration with Nazis had saved people with connections at the expense of those with none.[123] The topic inspired novels by well-known Israeli writers Amos Elon and Neil Gordon, was the subject of a 1987 British play, and was portrayed in a 1994 Israeli docudrama. [124]

Some Zionist leaders worked out what became known as the "transfer agreement," a 1933 pact with the Nazis in which Jews who wished to go to Palestine could transfer their capital to Palestine.[125] As part of this agreement, these Zionists agreed to reject a boycott that had been implemented against Germany.[126]

Critics were outraged at their undermining of the boycott, a fellow Zionist calling them "Hitler's allies."[127] According to author Edwin Black, "The great irony is that Adolph Hitler became the chief economic sponsor of Israel."[128]

Israeli author Tom Segev explains that the agreement "was based on the complementary interests of the German government and the Zionist movement: the Nazis wanted the Jews out of Germany; the Zionists wanted them to come to Palestine."[129]

For a time, the Nazis worked with these Zionist leaders to promote Jewish emigration to Palestine. A series in a Berlin paper published by Nazi propaganda minister Josef Goebbels was entitled "A Nazi Visits Palestine" and depicted glowing photographs of Jewish immigrants in Palestine. Goebbels created a medal with a swastika on one side and the Star of David on the other.[130]

Nazi official Adolph Eichmann (later famous for his public trial in Israel) learned some Hebrew and Yiddish and briefly visited Palestine in 1937. He met with Zionist leaders on a number of occasions, including meeting with Ben-Gurion chief assistant and future mayor of Jerusalem, Teddy Kollek. Eichmann's autobiography was never published and reportedly remains sealed somewhere in Israeli archives. [131]

As already referred to earlier, Zionist leader Samuel Landman in 1936 used a particularly ironic strategy to push for Britain's help in opening up Palestine to the growing number of Jewish refugees from Germany.

According to Landman, Zionist actions were responsible for the U.S. entry into World War I on the side of Britain. U.S. involvement then enabled the Allies to defeat Germany. The knowledge of this Zionist connection, Landman said, was a cause of the growing anti-Semitism in Germany. Therefore, Landsman argued, there was a greater need than ever for the Jewish state in Palestine that the British had allegedly promised in return for Jewish help in winning the war.[132]

Zionists fake "hate" attacks on Iraqi Jews

While Zionists wished for a massive "in-gathering of Jews" in one state, most Iraqi Jews wanted nothing to do with it, according to Iraq's then-Chief Rabbi, who stated: "Iraqi Jews will be forever against Zionism."

"Jews and Arabs have enjoyed the same rights and privileges for 1,000 years and do not regard themselves as a distinctive separate part of this nation," the rabbi declared.[133]

Zionists worked to change that by covertly attacking Iraqi Jews so as to induce them to "flee" to Israel. Zionists planted bombs in Iraqi synagogues and in the U.S. Information Service Library in Iraq "in attempts to portray the Iraqis as anti-American and to terrorize the Jews," according to author and former CIA operative Wilbur Crane Eveland.[134]

"Soon leaflets began to appear urging Jews to flee to Israel," writes Eveland, and "... most of the world believed reports that Arab terrorism had motivated the flight of the Iraqi Jews whom the Zionists had 'rescued' really just in order to increase Israel's Jewish population."[135]

Similarly, Naeim Giladi, a Jewish-Iraqi author who later lived in Israel and the U.S., describes this program from the inside: "I write about what the first prime minister of Israel called 'cruel Zionism.' I write about it because I was part of it."

Giladi states that "Jews from Islamic lands did not emigrate willingly to Israel." In order "to force them to leave," Giladi writes, "Jews killed Jews." He goes on to say that in an effort "to buy time to confiscate ever more Arab lands, Jews on numerous occasions rejected genuine peace initiatives from their Arab neighbors."[136]

Chapter Seven

THE MODERN ISRAEL LOBBY IS BORN

In the 1920s and 1930s, American Zionists retreated somewhat from overtly pushing for a Jewish state in Palestine. Instead, many focused on creating Jewish institutions in Palestine, reports historian Naomi Cohen, who calls this approach "Palestinianism." [137]

Cohen attributes this switch to American anti-Semitism in the 1920s and the Great Depression in the 1930s, but Americans' revulsion against militant nationalisms (particularly strong after WWI) must certainly have been an important factor.

Cohen writes that this retreat from overt Zionism "permitted the spread of a 'quiet' Zionism in synagogues and Jewish schools."[138]

Meanwhile, by not publicly declaring the end goal of a Jewish state, Zionists could avoid the appearance of "disloyalty or dual allegiance."[139] This better fit the temper of the times, following a war allegedly fought for democracy. A number of both Jewish and non-Jewish writers opposed the non-democratic agenda of creating a

Jewish state on land whose population was overwhelmingly non-Jewish.

As a Jewish writer pointed out in a Zionist journal, "...forcing foreign rule upon the majority of the population so that a minority may achieve political, economic and cultural privileges does not accord with the conscience of people bred in America and western Europe to the principles of free self-government."[140]

On the other hand, creating Jewish institutions in Palestine, such as the Hebrew University in Jerusalem, seemed to non-Zionists like altruism rather than the vanguard of a colonial movement. As Cohen explains, "To outsiders [non-Jewish Americans], it was basically a philanthropy, and Americans admired philanthropy and philanthropists."[141]

Zionist leaders felt that the US was critically important to their goal. Ben-Gurion, who had visited the United States almost every year after his election to the Zionist Executive, wrote in 1939 that he was convinced that "the main arena" for Zionist efforts outside Palestine should be America, stating that they had "no more effective tool at our disposal than the American Jewish community and Zionist Movement...."[142]

Zionist Moshe Shertok, a future Israeli foreign minister, stated during WWII, "America will have a decisive influence at the end of the war... and the question of our strength in America is a very real and important one."[143]

Shertok went on to state, "There are millions of active and well-organised Jews in America, and their position in life enables them to be most dynamic and influential. They live in the nerve-centres of the country, and hold important positions in politics, trade, journalism, the theatre and the radio. They could influence public opinion, but their strength is not felt, since it is not harnessed and directed at the right target."[144]

A Zionist leader decried what he considered a problem with American Jews at this time: "The American Jew thinks of himself first and foremost as an American citizen. This is a fact, whether we like it or not." He concluded, "Loyalty to America is now the supreme watchword."[145]

Zionists were determined to harness this untapped power, and soon the Zionist movement began to come into its own.

The immediate precursor to today's pro-Israel lobby began in 1939[146] under the leadership of Rabbi Abba Hillel Silver, originally from Lithuania. He created the American Zionist Emergency Council (AZEC), which by 1943 had acquired a budget of half a million dollars at a time when a nickel bought a loaf of bread.[147]

In addition to this money, Zionists had become influential in creating a fundraising umbrella organization, the United Jewish Appeal, in 1939[148], giving them access to the organization's gargantuan financial resources: $14 million in 1941, $150 million by 1948. This was four times more than Americans contributed to the Red Cross and was the equivalent of approximately $1.5 billion today.[149]

With its extraordinary funding, AZEC embarked on a campaign to target every sector of American society, ordering that local committees be set up in every Jewish community in the nation. In the words of AZEC organizer Sy Kenen, it launched "a political and public relations offensive to capture the support of Congressmen, clergy, editors, professors, business and labor."[150]

AZEC instructed activists to "make direct contact with your local Congressman or Senator" and to go after union members, wives and parents of servicemen, and Jewish war veterans. AZEC provided activists with form letters to use and schedules of anti-Zionist lecture tours to oppose and disrupt.

A measure of its power came in 1945 when Silver disliked a British move that would be harmful to Zionists. AZEC booked Madison Square Garden, ordered advertisements, and mailed 250,000 announcements – the first day. By the second day they had organized demonstrations in 30 cities, a letter-writing campaign, and convinced 27 U.S. Senators to give speeches.[151]

Grassroots Zionist action groups were organized with more than 400 local committees under 76 state and regional branches. AZEC funded books, articles and academic studies; millions of pamphlets were distributed. There were massive petition and letter writing campaigns. AZEC targeted college presidents and deans, managing to get more than 150 to sign one petition.[152]

Rabbi Elmer Berger, executive director of the American Council for Judaism, which opposed Zionism in the 1940s and '50s, writes in his memoirs that there was a "ubiquitous propaganda campaign reaching just about every point of political leverage in the country."[153]

The Zionist Organization of America bragged of the "immensity of our operations and their diversity" in its 48th Annual Report, stating, "We reach into every department of American life…"[154]

Berger and other anti-Zionist Jewish Americans tried to organize against "the deception and cynicism with which the Zionist machine operated," but failed to obtain anywhere near their level of funding. Among other things, would-be dissenters were afraid of "the savagery of personal attacks" anti-Zionists endured.[155]

Berger writes that when he and a colleague opposed a Zionist resolution in Congress, Emanuel Celler, a New York Democrat who was to serve in Congress for almost 50 years, told them: "They ought to take you b…s out and shoot you."[156]

When it was unclear that President Harry Truman would support Zionism, Cellar and a committee of Zionists told him that they had persuaded Dewey to support the Zionist policy and demanded that Truman also take this stand. Cellar reportedly pounded on Truman's table and said that if Truman did not do so, "We'll run you out of town.[157]

Jacob Javits, another well-known senator, this time Republican, told a Zionist women's group: "We'll fight to death and make a Jewish State in Palestine if it's the last thing that we do."[158]

Richard Stevens, author of *American Zionism and U.S. Foreign Policy, 1942-1947*, reports that Zionists infiltrated the boards of several Jewish schools that they felt didn't sufficiently promote the Zionist cause. When this didn't work, Stevens writes, they would start their own pro-Zionist schools.[159]

Stevens writes that in 1943-44 the ZOA distributed over a million leaflets and pamphlets to public libraries, chaplains, community centers, educators, ministers, writers and "others who might further the Zionist cause."[160]

Alfred Lilienthal, who had worked in the State Department, served in the U.S. Army in the Middle East from 1943-45, and became a member of the anti-Zionist American Council for Judaism, reports that Zionist monthly sales of books totaled between 3,000 and 4,000 throughout 1944-45.

Richard Stevens reports that Zionists subsidized books by non-Jewish authors that supported the Zionist agenda. They would then promote these books jointly with commercial publishers. Several of them became best sellers.[161]

Zionists manufacture Christian support

AZEC founder Silver and other Zionists played a significant role in creating Christian support for Zionism, a project Brandeis encouraged.[162]

Secret Zionist funds, eventually reaching $150,000 in 1946, were used to revive an elitist Protestant group, the American Palestine Committee. This group had originally been founded in 1932 by Emanuel Neumann, a member of the Executive of the Zionist Organization. The objective was to organize a group of prominent (mainly non-Jewish) Americans in moral and political support of Zionism. Frankfurter was one of the main speakers at its launch.[163]

Silver's headquarters issued a directive saying, "In every community an American Christian Palestine Committee must be immediately organized."[164]

Author Peter Grose reports that the Christian committee's operations "were hardly autonomous. Zionist headquarters thought nothing of placing newspaper advertisements on the clergymen's behalf without bothering to consult them in advance, until one of the committee's leaders meekly asked at least for prior notice before public statements were made in their name."[165]

AZEC formed another group among clergymen, the Christian Council on Palestine. An internal AZEC memo stated that the aim of both groups was to "crystallize the sympathy of Christian America for our cause."[166]

By the end of World War II the Christian Council on Palestine had grown to 3,000 members and the American Palestine Committee boasted a membership of 6,500 public figures, including senators, congressmen, cabinet members, governors, state officers, mayors, jurists, clergymen, educators, writers, publishers, and civic and industrial leaders.

Historian Richard Stevens explains that Christian support was largely gained by exploiting their wish to help people in need. Steven writes that Zionists would proclaim "the tragic plight of refugees fleeing from persecution and finding no home," thus linking the refugee problem with Palestine as allegedly the only solution.[167]

Stevens writes that the reason for this strategy was clear: "…while many Americans might not support the creation of a Jewish state, traditional American humanitarianism could be exploited in favor of the Zionist cause through the refugee problems."[168]

Few if any of these Christian supporters had any idea that the creation of the Jewish state would entail a massive expulsion of hundreds of thousands of non-Jews, who made up the large majority of Palestine's population, creating a new and much longer lasting refugee problem.

Nor did they learn that during and after Israel's founding 1947-49 war, Zionist forces attacked a number of Christian sites. Donald Neff, former *Time Magazine* Jerusalem bureau chief and author of five books on Israel-Palestine, reports in detail on Zionist attacks on Christian sites in May 1948, the month of Israel's birth.

Neff tells us that a group of Christian leaders complained that month that Zionists had killed and wounded hundreds of people, including children, refugees and clergy, at Christian churches and humanitarian institutions.

For example, the group charged that "'many children were killed or wounded' by Jewish shells on the Convent of Orthodox Copts…; eight refugees were killed and about 120 wounded at the Orthodox Armenian Convent…; and that Father Pierre Somi, secretary to the Bishop, had been killed and two wounded at the Orthodox Syrian Church of St. Mark."

"The group's statement said Arab forces had abided by their promise to respect Christian institutions, but that the Jews had forcefully occupied Christian structures and been indiscriminate in shelling churches," reports Neff. He quotes a Catholic priest: "'Jewish soldiers broke down the doors of my church and robbed many precious and sacred objects. Then they threw the statues of Christ down into a nearby garden.' [The priest] added that Jewish leaders had reassured that religious buildings would be respected, 'but their deeds do not correspond to their words.'"[169]

After Zionist soldiers invaded and looted a convent in Tiberias, the U.S. Consulate sent a bitter dispatch back to the State Department complaining of "the Jewish attitude in Jerusalem towards Christian institutions."[170]

An American Christian Biblical scholar concurred, reporting that a friend in Jerusalem had been told, "When we get control you can take your dead Christ and go home."[171]

Chapter Eight

ZIONIST COLONIZATION EFFORTS IN PALESTINE

As early Zionists in the U.S. and elsewhere pushed for the creation of a Jewish state, Zionists in Palestine simultaneously tried to clear the land of Muslim and Christian inhabitants and replace them with Jewish immigrants.

This was a tall order, as Muslims and Christians accounted for more than 95 percent of the population of Palestine.[172] Zionists planned to try first to buy up the land until the previous inhabitants had emigrated; failing this, they would use violence to force them out. This dual strategy was discussed in various written documents cited by numerous Palestinian and Israeli historians.[173]

As this colonial project grew, the indigenous Palestinians reacted with occasional bouts of violence; Zionists had anticipated this since people usually resist being expelled from their land.

When the buyout effort was able to obtain only a few percent of the land, Zionists created a number of terrorist groups to fight against both the Palestinians and the British. Terrorist and future Israeli Prime Minister Menachem Begin later bragged that Zionists had brought terrorism both to the Middle East and to the world at large.[174]

By the eve of the creation of Israel, the Zionist immigration and buyout project had increased the Jewish population of Palestine to 30 percent[175] and land ownership from 1 percent to approximately 6-7 percent.[176]

This was in 1947, when the British at last announced that they would end their control of Palestine. Britain turned the territory's fate over to the United Nations.

Since a founding principle of the UN was "self-determination of peoples," one would have expected to the UN to support fair, democratic elections in which inhabitants could create their own independent country.[177]

Instead, Zionists pushed for a General Assembly resolution to give them a disproportionate 55 percent of Palestine.[178][179] (While they rarely announced this publicly, their plan, stated in journal entries and letters, was to later take the rest of Palestine.[180])

U.S. Officials oppose creation of Israel

The U.S. State Department opposed this partition plan strenuously, considering Zionism contrary to both fundamental American principles and U.S. interests.

For example, the director of the State Department's Office of Near Eastern and African Affairs consistently recommended against supporting a Jewish state in Palestine. The director, named Loy Henderson, warned that the creation of such a state would go against locals' wishes, imperil U.S. interests and violate democratic principles.

Henderson emphasized that the U.S. would lose moral standing in the world if it supported Zionism:

"At the present time the United States has a moral prestige in the Near and Middle East unequaled by that of any other great power. We would lose that prestige and would be likely for many years to be considered as a betrayer of the high principles which we ourselves have enunciated during the period of the [second world] war."[181]

When Zionists pushed the partition plan in the UN, Henderson recommended strongly against supporting their proposal, saying that such a partition would have to be implemented by force and was "not based on any principle." He warned that partition "would guarantee that the Palestine problem would be permanent and still more complicated in the future…"

Henderson elaborated further on how plans to partition Palestine would violate American and UN principles:

"…[Proposals for partition] are in definite contravention to various principles laid down in the [UN] Charter as well as to principles on which American concepts of Government are based. These proposals, for instance, ignore such principles as self-determination and majority rule. They recognize the principle of a theocratic racial state and even go so far in several instances as to discriminate on grounds of religion and race…"[182]

Zionists attacked Henderson virulently, calling him "anti-Semitic," demanding his resignation, and threatening his family. They pressured the State Department to transfer him elsewhere; one analyst describes this as "the historic game of musical chairs" in which officials who recommended Middle East policies "consistent with the nation's interests" were moved on.[183]

In 1948 Truman sent Henderson to the slopes of the Himalayas, as Ambassador to Nepal (then officially under India).[184] (In recent years, at times virtually every State Department country desk has been directed by a Zionist.)[185]

But Henderson was far from alone in making his recommendations. He wrote that his views were not only those of the entire Near East Division but were shared by "nearly every member of the Foreign Service or of the [State] Department who has worked to any appreciable extent on Near Eastern problems."[186]

He wasn't exaggerating. Official after official and agency after agency opposed Zionism.

In 1947 the CIA reported that Zionist leadership was pursuing objectives that would endanger both Jews and "the strategic interests of the Western powers in the Near and Middle East."[187]

Ambassador Henry F. Grady, who has been called "America's top diplomatic soldier for a critical period of the Cold War," headed a 1946 commission aimed at coming up with a solution for Palestine. Grady later wrote about the Zionist lobby and its damaging effect on U.S. national interests.

"I have had a good deal of experience with lobbies but this group started where those of my experience had ended," wrote Grady. "I have headed a number of government missions but in no other have I ever experienced so much disloyalty.... [I]n the United States, since there is no political force to counterbalance Zionism, its campaigns are apt to be decisive."[188]

Grady concluded that without Zionist pressure, the U.S. would not have had "the ill-will with the Arab states, which are of such strategic importance in our 'cold war' with the soviets."[189]

Former Undersecretary of State Dean Acheson also opposed Zionism. Acheson's biographer writes that Acheson "worried that the West would pay a high price for Israel." Another author, John Mulhall, records Acheson's warning of the danger for U.S. interests:

"...to transform [Palestine] into a Jewish State capable of receiving a million or more immigrants would vastly exacerbate the political problem and imperil not only American but all Western interests in the Near East."[190]

The Joint Chiefs of Staff reported in late 1947, "A decision to partition Palestine, if the decision were supported by the United States, would prejudice United States strategic interests in the Near and Middle East" to the point that "United States influence in the area would be curtailed to that which could be maintained by military force."[191]

The Joint Chiefs issued at least sixteen papers on the Palestine issue following World War II. They were particularly concerned that the Zionist goal was to involve the U.S.

One 1948 paper predicted that "the Zionist strategy will seek to involve [the United States] in a continuously widening and deepening series of operations intended to secure maximum Jewish objectives."[192]

The CIA stated that Zionist leadership was pursuing objectives that would endanger both Jews and "the

47

strategic interests of the Western powers in the Near and Middle East."[193]

The head of the State Department's Division of Near Eastern Affairs, Gordon P. Merriam, warned against the partition plan on moral grounds:

"U.S. support for partition of Palestine as a solution to that problem can be justified only on the basis of Arab and Jewish consent. Otherwise we should violate the principle of self-determination which has been written into the Atlantic Charter, the declaration of the United Nations, and the United Nations Charter – a principle that is deeply embedded in our foreign policy. Even a United Nations determination in favor of partition would be, in the absence of such consent, a stultification and violation of UN's own charter." [194]

Merriam added that without consent, "bloodshed and chaos" would follow, a tragically accurate prediction.

An internal State Department memorandum accurately predicted how Israel would be born through armed aggression masked as defense:

"...the Jews will be the actual aggressors against the Arabs. However, the Jews will claim that they are merely defending the boundaries of a state which were traced by the UN.... In the event of such Arab outside aid the Jews will come running to the Security Council with the claim that their state is the object of armed aggression and will use every means to obscure the fact that it is their own armed aggression against the Arabs inside which is the cause of Arab counter-attack."[195]

And American Vice Consul William J. Porter foresaw one last outcome of the "partition" plan: that no Arab state would actually ever come to be in Palestine.[196]

Chapter Nine

TRUMAN ACCEDES TO PRO-ISRAEL LOBBY

President Harry Truman, however, ignored this advice and chose instead to support the Zionist partition plan. Truman's political advisor, Clark Clifford, believed that the Jewish vote and contributions were essential to winning the upcoming presidential election, and that supporting the partition plan would garner that support. (Truman's opponent, Dewey, took similar stands for similar reasons.)[197]

Truman's Secretary of State George Marshall, the renowned World War II General and author of the Marshall Plan, was furious to see electoral considerations taking precedence over policies based on national interest. He condemned what he called a "transparent dodge to win a few votes," which would make "[t]he great dignity of the office of President seriously diminished."[198]

Marshall wrote that the counsel offered by Clifford "was based on domestic political considerations, while the problem which confronted us was international. I said bluntly that if the President were to follow Mr. Clifford's advice and if in the elections I were to vote, I would vote against the President..."[199]

Secretary of Defense James Forrestal also tried, unsuccessfully, to oppose the Zionists. He was outraged that Truman's Mideast policy was based on what he called "squalid political purposes," asserting that "United States policy should be based on United States national interests and not on domestic political considerations."[200]

Forrestal represented the general Pentagon view when he said that "no group in this country should be permitted to influence our policy to the point where it could endanger our national security."[201]

A report by the National Security Council warned that the Palestine turmoil was acutely endangering the security of the United States. A CIA report stressed the strategic importance of the Middle East and its oil resources.[202]

Similarly, George F. Kennan, the State Department's Director of Policy Planning, issued a top-secret document on January 19, 1947 that outlined the enormous damage done to the U.S. by the partition plan ("Report by the Policy Planning Staff on Position of the United States with Respect to Palestine").[203]

Kennan cautioned that "important U.S. oil concessions and air base rights" could be lost through U.S. support for partition and warned that the USSR stood to gain by the partition plan.

Kermit Roosevelt, Theodore Roosevelt's grandson and a legendary intelligence agent, was another who was deeply disturbed by events, noting:

"The process by which Zionist Jews have been able to promote American support for the partition of Palestine demonstrates the vital need of a foreign policy based on national rather than partisan interests…. Only when the national interests of the United States, in their highest terms, take precedence over all other considerations, can a logical, farseeing foreign policy be evolved. No American political leader has the right to compromise American interests to gain partisan votes…"[204]

Kermit Roosevelt went on:

"The present course of world crisis will increasingly force upon Americans the realization that their national interests and those of the proposed Jewish state in Palestine are going to conflict. It is to be hoped that American Zionists and non-Zionists alike will come to grips with the realities of the problem."[205]

Truman wrote in his memoirs: "I do not think I ever had as much pressure and propaganda aimed at the White House as I had in this instance." There were now about a million dues-paying Zionists in the U.S.[206]

Then, as now, in addition to unending pressure there was financial compensation, Truman reportedly receiving a suitcase full of money from Zionists while on his train campaign around the country.[207]

Personal influences on Truman

One person key in such Zionist financial connections to Truman was Abraham Feinberg, a wealthy businessman who was later to play a similar role with President Johnson.[208]

While many Americans have been aware of Truman's come-from-behind win over Dewey, few people know about the critical role of Feinberg and the Zionist lobby in financing Truman's victory. After Feinberg financed Truman's famous whistle-stop campaign tour, Truman credited him with his presidential win.[209] (When the CIA later discovered that Feinberg also helped to finance illegal gun-running to Zionist groups, the Truman administration looked the other way.[210])

An individual inside the U.S. government who worked to influence policy was David K. Niles, executive assistant first to FDR and then to Truman. Niles, according to author Alfred Lilienthal, was "a member of a select group of confidential advisers with an often-quoted passion for anonymity. Niles… though occasionally publicized as Mr. Truman's Mystery Man, remained totally unknown to the public."[211]

Behind the scenes Niles was regularly briefed by the head of the Washington Office of the Zionist Organization of America (ZOA).[212]

When it was discovered that top-secret information was being passed on to the Israeli government, Chairman of the Joint Chiefs of Staff General Omar Bradley told Truman he had to choose between Bradley and Niles. Not long after, Niles resigned and went on a visit to Israel.[213]

Another who helped influence Truman was his old Kansas City friend and business partner, Eddie Jacobson, active in B'nai B'rith and "a passionate believer in Jewish nationalism," who was able to procure Zionist access to the President at key times.[214] Truman called Jacobson's input of "decisive importance."[215]

Still another was Sam Rosenman, a political advisor to Truman, who screened State Department memos sent to Truman. A longtime diplomat reports that one of the department's memoranda was returned, unopened, with a notation, "President Truman already knows your views and doesn't need this."[216]

Evan M. Wilson, a career diplomat who had been U.S. Consul General in Jerusalem, later wrote that Truman had been largely motivated by "domestic political considerations."[217] At least one of Truman's key policy speeches was drafted primarily by the Washington representative of the Jewish Agency.[218]

Under Secretary of State James E. Webb in a dispatch to Secretary of State Dean Acheson noted the obvious: "Past record suggests Israel has had more influence with U.S. than has U.S. with Israel."[219]

Chapter Ten

PRO-ISRAEL PRESSURE ON GENERAL ASSEMBLY MEMBERS

When it was clear that, despite U.S. support,[220] the partition recommendation did not have the two-thirds support of the UN General Assembly required to pass, Zionists pushed through a delay in the vote. They then used this period to pressure numerous nations into voting for the recommendation. A number of people later described this campaign.

Robert Nathan, a Zionist who had worked for the U.S. government and who was particularly active in the Jewish Agency, wrote afterward, "We used any tools at hand," such as telling certain delegations that the Zionists would use their influence to block economic aid to any countries that did not vote for partition.[221]

Another Zionist proudly stated:

"Every clue was meticulously checked and pursued. Not the smallest or the remotest of nations, but was contacted and wooed. Nothing was left to chance."

Financier and longtime presidential advisor Bernard Baruch told France it would lose U.S. aid if it voted against partition. Top White House presidential aide David Niles organized pressure on Liberia through rubber magnate Harvey Firestone, who told the Liberian president that if Liberia did not vote in favor of partition, Firestone would revoke his planned expansion in the country. Liberia voted yes.[222]

Latin American delegates were told that the Pan-American highway construction project would be more likely if they voted yes. Delegates' wives received mink coats (the wife of the Cuban delegate returned hers); Costa Rica's President Jose Figueres reportedly received a blank checkbook. Haiti was promised economic aid if it would change its original vote opposing partition.

Longtime Zionist Supreme Court Justice Felix Frankfurter, along with ten senators and Truman domestic advisor Clark Clifford, threatened the Philippines (seven bills on the Philippines were pending in Congress).

Before the vote on the plan, the Philippine delegate had given a passionate speech against partition, defending the inviolable "primordial rights of a people to determine their political future and to preserve the territorial integrity of their native land..."[223]

The delegate went on to say that he could not believe that the General Assembly would sanction a move that would place the world "back on the road to the dangerous principles of racial exclusiveness and to the archaic documents of theocratic governments."

Twenty-four hours later, after intense Zionist pressure, the Philippine delegate voted in favor of partition.[224]

On Nov 29, 1947, UN General Assembly Resolution 181, the resolution creating partition, passed. While this resolution is frequently cited, it was of limited (if any) legal impact. General Assembly resolutions, unlike Security Council resolutions, are not binding on member states. For this reason, the resolution requested that "[t]he Security Council take the necessary measures as provided for in the plan for its implementation,"[225] which the Security Council never did. Legally, the General Assembly Resolution was a "recommendation" and did not create any states.[226]

What it did do, however, was increase the fighting in Palestine. Within months the Zionists had forced out over 413,000 people.[227] Zionist military units had stealthily been preparing for war before the UN vote and had acquired massive weaponry, some of it through a widespread network of illicit gunrunning operations in the U.S. under a number of front groups. (See below)

On May 15th Zionists announced the creation of their new state. They decided to name it "Israel," and chose not to set its boundaries or to write a Constitution (a situation that continues through today). Five Arab armies joined the fighting, but, contrary to general perceptions of this war, Zionist/Israeli forces outnumbered the combined Arab and Palestinian combatants.[228]

The UN eventually managed to create a temporary and very partial ceasefire, during which Israel obtained even more armaments. A Swedish UN mediator, Count Folke Bernadotte, who had previously rescued thousands of Jews from the Nazis,[229] was dispatched to negotiate an end to the violence. Israeli assassins killed him and Israel continued what it was to call its "war of independence."[230]

At the end of this war, through ruthless implementation of plans to push out as many non-Jews as possible, Israel came into existence on 78 percent of Palestine.[231]

But let us take a closer look at the violence that followed the UN recommendation.

Chapter Eleven

MASSACRES AND THE CONQUEST OF PALESTINE

The passing of the partition resolution in November 1947 triggered the violence that State Department and Pentagon analysts had predicted and for which Zionists had been preparing. There were at least 33 massacres of Palestinian villages, half of them before a single Arab army joined the conflict.[232] Zionist forces were better equipped and had more men under arms than their opponents[233] and by the end of Israel's "War of Independence" over 750,000 Palestinian men, women, and children were ruthlessly expelled.[234] Zionists had succeeded in the first half of their goal: Israel, the self-described Jewish State, had come into existence.[235]

As Israeli historian Tom Segev writes, "Israel was born of terror, war, and revolution, and its creation required a measure of fanaticism and cruelty."[236]

The massacres were carried out by Zionist forces, including Zionist militias that had engaged in terrorist attacks in the area for years preceding the partition resolution.[237]

Descriptions of the massacres, by both Palestinians and Israelis, are nightmarish. An Israeli eyewitness reported that at the village of al-Dawayima:

"The children they killed by breaking their heads with sticks. There was not a house without dead....One soldier boasted that he had raped a woman and then shot her."[238]

One Palestinian woman testified that a man shot her nine-month-pregnant sister and then cut her stomach open with a butcher knife.[239]

One of the better-documented massacres occurred in a small, neutral Palestinian village called Deir Yassin in April 1948 – before any Arab armies had joined the war. A Swiss Red Cross representative was one of the first to arrive on the scene, where he found 254 dead, including 145 women, 35 of them pregnant. [240]

Witnesses reported that the attackers lined up families – men, women, grandparents and children, even infants – and shot them. [241]

An eyewitness and future colonel in the Israeli military later wrote of the militia members: "They didn't know how to fight, but as murderers they were pretty good."[242]

The Red Cross representative who found the bodies at Deir Yassin arrived in time to see some of the killing in action. He wrote in his diary that Zionist militia members were still entering houses with guns and knives when he arrived. He saw one young Jewish woman carrying a blood-covered dagger and saw another stab an old couple in their doorway. The representative wrote that the scene reminded him of S.S. troops he had seen in Athens.[243]

Richard Catling, British assistant inspector general for the criminal investigation division, reported on "sexual atrocities" committed by Zionist forces. "Many young school girls were raped and later slaughtered," he reported. "Old women were also molested."[244]

The Deir Yassin attack was perpetrated by two Zionist militias and coordinated with the main Zionist forces, whose elite unit participated in part of the operation.[245] The heads of the two militias, Menachem Begin and Yitzhak Shamir, later became Prime Ministers of Israel.

Begin, head of the Irgun militia, sent the following message to his troops about their victory at Deir Yassin:

"Accept my congratulations on this splendid act of conquest. Convey my regards to all the commanders and soldiers. We shake your hands. We are all proud of the excellent leadership and the fighting spirit in this great attack. We stand to attention in memory of the slain. We lovingly shake the hands of the wounded. Tell the soldiers: you have made history in Israel with your attack and your conquest. Continue thus until victory. As in Deir Yassin, so everywhere, we will attack and smite the enemy. God, God, Thou has chosen us for conquest."[246]

Approximately six months later, Begin (who had also publicly taken credit for other terrorist acts, including blowing up the King David Hotel [247] in Jerusalem, killing 91 people) came on a tour of America. The tour's sponsors included famous playwright Ben Hecht, a fervent Zionist who applauded Irgun violence,[248] and eventually included 11 Senators, 12 governors, 70 Congressmen, 17 Justices, and numerous other public officials.[249]

The State Department, fully aware of his violent activities in Palestine, tried to reject Begin's visa but was overruled by Truman.[250]

Begin later proudly admitted his terrorism in an interview for American television. When the interviewer asked him, "How does it feel, in the light of all that's going on, to be the father of terrorism in the Middle East?" Begin proclaimed, "In the Middle East? In all the world!"[251]

Chapter Twelve

U.S. FRONT GROUPS FOR ZIONIST MILITARISM

A number of groups operated in the U.S. to support Zionist paramilitary groups in Palestine. These often employed clandestine methods and deceptive names. The general American public had little idea about the true nature of these groups and what they were supporting.

a. Irgun Delegation: Hillel Kook as "Peter Bergson"

A covert Irgun delegation operated in the U.S. from the late 1930s through 1948 under a half dozen front organizations, including the "Emergency Committee to Save European Jewry" and "American Friends of a Jewish Palestine."[252]

The main leader was Hillel Kook, the senior Irgun officer working outside Palestine. Upon coming to the U.S. he assumed the alias "Peter Bergson," and the group is often called the "Bergson Boys."

The other leader was Yitzhak Ben-Ami (father of Jeremy Ben-Ami, founder of today's lobbying organization

J-Street). Also closely involved was Eri Jabotinski, son of right-wing Zionist leader Vladimir "Ze'ev" Jabotinsky.[253] Also associated with the group was Meir Kahane, who twenty years later founded the violent Jewish Defense League (JDL).[254]

Though historians have documented that their purpose in coming to the U.S. was to raise money for Irgun activities in Palestine, this was unknown to the multitude of high-level supporters the group eventually acquired. These supporters included Eleanor Roosevelt,[255] Harry Truman, Dorothy Parker, Herbert Hoover, Will Rogers, Jr., Labor leader William Green, U.S. Solicitor General Fowler Harper, and U.S. Interior Secretary Harold Ickes.[256]

The FBI, however, suspected this illegal fundraising. It investigated the front groups several times, but largely bungled the investigations and failed to produce evidence. As author Rafael Medoff divulges: "In fact, according to Bergson lobbyist Baruch Rabinowitz, funds raised by the Bergsonites in the United States were indeed secretly transferred to the Irgun; the methods of transfer were simply so well concealed that the FBI could not uncover them."[257]

Their biographer, Israeli professor Judith Baumel, writes that the Irgun Delegation quickly set about "integrating themselves into the social and political culture of their temporary home." They quickly grasped that "public mood, molded to a large extent by propaganda and public relations [was] a dominant force in the American system of direct representation" and they soon became masters of media manipulation.[258]

Thus, besides their secret funneling of money for terrorist activities in Palestine against Palestinians, the

British, and members of the Jewish community[259], the Irgun Delegation engaged in numerous public activities pushing for the Jewish state in Palestine. They lobbied Congress and the White House, organized a march on Washington, D.C. of 500 Rabbis, and placed full-page ads in newspapers around the U.S.

They also produced a pageant called "We Will Never Die!" celebrating the Jewish contribution to Western civilization, written by Ben Hecht, directed by Moss Hart, featuring music by Kurt Weil, and starring Edward G. Robinson. The cast also included Dean Martin, Frank Sinatra, Leonard Bernstein, one hundred Yeshiva students from Brooklyn, and fifty Orthodox rabbis.[260] Forty thousand attended the extravaganza's New York performances. It then went on to play in most of America's largest cities. The group produced several other plays and rallies, one of which starred a young Marlon Brando and brought in $1 million.

Baumel reports that an American Jewish leader who had immigrated to Palestine wrote to Eleanor Roosevelt asking her to withdraw support from the Brando production, because its profits "were being used to fund terrorist activity."[261] Eleanor ignored this advice, apparently unaware that it was well founded.

During WWII, the various organizations created by the Irgun Delegation frequently pushed for rescuing European Jews from the Nazis, but one of their major demands was for the creation of a "Jewish Army of Stateless and Palestinian Jews." The idea was that the Allies should create a Jewish army to fight alongside them against the Nazis.

However, certain right-wing Zionists had sought this army even before the Nazi holocaust began, and some analysts argue it was a plan with a mixed agenda.[262] Historian William Rubinstein writes, "It is rather difficult to believe that Bergson's implausible proposal did not have far more to do with creating the nucleus of a Jewish Palestinian force, to be used against the British and the Arabs, than with saving Europe's Jews from the Nazis."[263]

One supporter, best-selling author Pierre van Paassen, resigned when he learned that various Delegation-spawned "committees" to save Jews were all being run by the same small group, and that they were tied to horrific terrorist actions in Palestine.

He declared that he did not believe they had the means or intention to truly save Jews from the Nazis, writing: "To speak bluntly, that 'Committee to Save the Jewish People of Europe' is a hoax, in my judgment a very cruel hoax perpetrated on the American public, Jewish and non-Jewish alike."[264]

Some at the time and since have considered the Delegation's efforts heroic, but critics point out that it did not manage to rescue any Jews during the Nazi holocaust[265], though it may have helped contribute to the pressure on President Roosevelt to later create a War Refugee Board.[266]

The group had numerous opponents among Jewish leaders, both Zionist and anti-Zionist.[267] Some, unlike the general public, were aware of their secret connections to Menachem Begin's Irgun, whose violent tactics many found abhorrent, particularly when they targeted the British at a time that England was fighting to defeat Hitler – the most effective way, many felt, to rescue Jews.

Biographer Baumel writes that the more mainstream Zionist establishment was disturbed by "the clandestine nature of the committee's formation and the absence of any hint as to its intention."[268]

This division among Zionists was largely hidden from view, however, as the Delegation aimed for the American man in the street, using tantalizing slogans, illustrated advertisements, and "seductive curiosity-whetting gimmicks." Baumel notes that the Irgun Delegation's primary triumph was to understand "the power of Madison Avenue."[269]

Author Rafael Medoff describes the importance of that understanding: "[T]he violent behavior of the Jewish forces in Palestine would have surely undermined American public sympathy for the Zionist cause, if not for the efforts of the Jewish underground's American friends."[270] This public relations crusade was critical in building American support.

After WWII, the Delegation became involved in the sometimes secretive, sometimes very public movement of European Jews to Palestine. One purpose, Ben-Ami explained, was to build up the Irgun terror forces: "We must build a network in Europe capable of moving thousands of Irgun soldiers to Palestine..."[271] This intention, however, was not announced to the general public.

Bergson-Kook's uncle was Rabbi Avraham Yitzhak Kook, often known as "Rabbi Kook the Elder." Rabbi Kook was originally from Eastern Europe, had worked toward the Balfour Declaration in Britain,[272] and eventually became the "Chief Rabbi of Palestine."

Perhaps his most significant accomplishment was to devise an ideology that merged a Kabbalistic version of religious Judaism with political Zionism, founding an extremist religious Zionism that continues in existence today.[273]

The Kabala teaches that non-Jews are the embodiment of Satan, and that the world was created solely for the sake of Jews.[274] Rabbi Kook, who achieved saintly status among his followers in Israel and the U.S., stated: "The difference between a Jewish soul and souls of non-Jews… is greater and deeper than the difference between a human soul and the souls of cattle."[275]

In addition to spanning the Jewish religious-secular continuum, the Irgun Delegation spanned the political spectrum from left to right. Baumel writes that it "evinced many of the unique characteristics of Eastern European protofascism" while also forming partnerships with communists and Jews who belonged to left-wing American groups.[276]

b. Rabbi Korff and the "Political Action Committee for Palestine"

Another terrorist front group and PR machine was formed by an Orthodox rabbi named Baruch Korff,[277] who achieved tremendous mainstream success and became well known in the U.S. His underground activities, on the other hand, were considerably less known.

Korff had earlier been executive director of one of the Bergson group's entities,[278] before starting his own splinter group, the Political Action Committee for Palestine (PACP). Korff used many of the same tactics as Kook, while also building close relationships with various active and former Congressmen.

Korff combined these strong political connections and PR machinations to extraordinary, if duplicitous, effect. One example, which historian Rafael Medoff calls "a particularly well choreographed stunt," involved a former Republican Congressman, Joseph Clark Baldwin of New York.

At Korff's request, Baldwin, who had friendly relations with President Truman, staged a highly publicized visit to England and Palestine in late 1946.[279]

Korff then composed "Baldwin's" official report of the visit, which called on England and the United States to recognize Palestine "as an independent democracy of which homeless European Jews shall be considered citizens."[280]

Then, immediately after writing Baldwin's report, Korff put out a press release criticizing one aspect of the report, in order to make it appear that Baldwin "was not a puppet of the PACP but rather had visited London and Jerusalem with an open mind and returned with his own conclusions."[281]

Korff was also involved in a terrorist plot that was foiled at the last minute by a young American World War II aviator studying in France.

British intelligence had discovered in 1946 that Jewish terrorists, including Korff, were planning to assassinate the British foreign minister. For some reason details about this were heavily censored from the British public for many years, but in 2003 the British security files were finally released.[282]

In 1947, Korff and his group hatched a plan to drop bombs on the British foreign office, along with 10,000 threatening leaflets. "[W]e will carry the war to the very heart of the [British] Empire," the leaflets were to read. "We will strike with all the bitterness and fury of our servitude and bondage."[283]

The group tried to recruit a young American aviator in Paris to fly a plane from which the bombs would be dropped, promising him "lucrative jobs" after the mission was completed.[284] The aviator, Reginald Gilbert, had flown 136 combat missions over Europe during WWII, shooting down three German planes and damaging seven.

Gilbert pretended to agree to the plot, but instead informed the American Embassy, and then worked with Scotland Yard and the Paris police to have the would-be assassins arrested. French police, who said they "feared for the flier's life if the Stern gang ever caught up with him," then flew him to London until he could return to the U.S.[285]

Almost no one remembers this plot today, but it was headline news at the time in newspapers across the United States.[286] While some news accounts revealed the full plot, reports quickly stopped mentioning the bombs and recounted only the plan to drop the threatening leaflets. Someone was leaning on spokespeople or reporters to make sure only part of the story got out.

But they couldn't keep Gilbert quiet. In a first-hand account of the plot published by the *New York Herald Tribune*, Gilbert confirmed that the group had planned much more than a leaflet drop. The first idea had been to drop bombs on Britain's Parliament, but the target was subsequently changed to the Foreign Ministry, "because

Korff held a grudge against that office for refusing him a visa to Palestine."[287]

In his article, Gilbert recounted a conversation he had with Korff while playing along with the plot, which he continued to do at the direction of the Paris police. He says he told Korff fog might prevent them from locating their exact target, to which Korff replied that they could just drop the bombs anywhere on London. When Gilbert protested that innocent people might be killed, Korff replied, "They are British, so they are our enemy."[288]

After being arrested by Paris police and charged with "illegal possession of explosives and war weapons",[289] Korff came up with various stories. At one point he claimed that Gilbert had been the guilty party. Next, he and Hillel Kook (using his alias "Peter Bergson") claimed that the plot was a British "frameup" and that Gilbert was a British agent.[290] In other versions, Korff claimed that the "British Nazi Party" fabricated the story,[291] a claim picked up by the British weekly *News Review*.[292]

According to the London *Times*, Korff later said that "millions of dollars had been subscribed by private American sources to fund the purchase of the aircraft."[293]

Powerful allies proclaimed that Korff was innocent and brought pressure on the State Department to help him.[294] These allies included Korff's contacts in Congress and his father, Rabbi Jacob Korff, who was leader of the Boston Jewish Rabbinate and wielded considerable influence (when he died, the Massachusetts governor and Boston mayor attended his funeral, which was accompanied by a 5,000-person march.)[295] By November 22nd all charges were dropped.

In 1948, Baruch Korff had the temerity to publish a large advertisement in the *New York Post* calling a State Department policy against enforcing the Partition of Palestine "pure and simple anti-Semitism… plain everyday anti-Semitism, incorporated in the hearts and minds of those who govern free America."[296]

Later, Korff became a close friend and fervent supporter of President Richard Nixon, who called him "my rabbi."[297] Korff is reported to have influenced Nixon's strong support for Israel and efforts to allow Soviet Jews to emigrate.[298] It appears that Nixon was unaware of Korff's terror-connected past. According to a book on Nixon by investigative reporters Bob Woodward and Carl Bernstein (who also appear to have been ignorant of Korff's background), Korff introduced himself to Nixon as a "just a small-town rabbi."[299]

Korff served as a chaplain for the Massachusetts Department of Mental Health for 21 years.[300] He later acted as a "consultant to Brown University in conjunction with the school's acquisition of his extensive archives."[301] According to the London *Independent,* Korff had many supporters in high places in Israel, including Prime Ministers Yitzhak Rabin and Golda Meir.[302]

c. The "Sonneborn Institute"

A third collective of front groups was the secret American arm of the main Zionist paramilitary in Palestine, the Haganah. Known as the "Sonneborn Institute," it was founded by an American, Rudolf G. Sonneborn, in conjunction David Ben-Gurion, who led Zionist forces in Palestine.[303]

Sonneborn, scion of a wealthy German-Jewish family from Baltimore, had met Ben-Gurion in 1919. Sonneborn had traveled to the Versailles peace conference as secretary of a Zionist delegation, at the behest of Supreme Court Justice Brandeis (a family friend), and afterward went on a tour of Palestine.[304]

In 1945, Sonneborn and Ben-Gurion hosted a meeting of seventeen well-connected guests at Sonneborn's Manhattan penthouse. Ben-Gurion informed the group that their purpose was to form an underground organization to raise money and support "for purposes which could not be publicized or even fully disclosed."

The guests came from Los Angeles, Toronto, Miami, Birmingham, Philadelphia, Pittsburgh, Cleveland, Columbus, Minneapolis, St. Louis, Newark, New Haven and New York. One was a rabbi, five were lawyers, and the others were highly successful businessmen.[305] The organization was eventually to have representatives in at least 35 to 40 industry groups, and in one month alone there were meetings in Memphis, Ohio, New Jersey, Cedar Rapids, Iowa City, Baton Rouge, Dallas, Washington DC, and 40 more were scheduled.

They also organized Zionist youth groups, whose young members sometimes helped load guns onto boats headed for Palestine for use in taking over the land for a Jewish state. [306]

U.S. authorities tried to stop these illegal and damaging activities. In 1948, the Director of Central Intelligence filed a top-secret report with the Secretary of Defense about the Zionist arms trafficking. He warned, "U.S. National security is unfavorably affected by these developments and it could be seriously jeopardized by continued illicit traffic in the 'implements of war.'"[307]

But, like the other Zionist front groups discussed above, the Sonneborn Institute had friends in high places. Author Grant Smith reports that, under Truman, "Haganah operative groups active in arms trafficking within the U.S., like the terrorist charges, would only be lightly investigated and seldom prosecuted."[308]

* * *

The amount of American money mobilized for Zionism during this period is impossible to know, but indications suggest that it was astronomical. The Jewish Agency for Israel raised the equivalent in today's dollars of $3.5 billion between 1939 and May 1948 alone. And, as has been described above, this was just one of numerous Zionist organizations raising money from Americans.[309]

Chapter Thirteen

INFILTRATING DISPLACED PERSON'S CAMPS IN EUROPE TO FUNNEL PEOPLE TO PALESTINE

A similar underground campaign was operating in Europe. Zionist cadres infiltrated displaced person's camps that had been set up to house refugees displaced during WWII. These infiltrators tried secretly to funnel people to Palestine. When it turned out that most didn't want to go to Palestine, they worked to convince them – sometimes by force.

The fact was that Zionists needed more people to go to Palestine. As Ben-Gurion stated in 1944: [T]he essence of Zionism is one of a populating endeavor, to populate [Israel] with multitudes of Jews."[310]

Israeli professor Yosef Grodzinsky explains that Zionists were looking for "*chomer 'enoshi tov* (good human materials, a phrase Zionist organizers frequently used). Convincing Jews to uproot themselves and move to Palestine proved to be a formidable task: When life is good, people tend to stay where they are. Candidates for Palestine immigration therefore had to be Jews whose life was not good. Post-Holocaust DPs [displaced persons], became a human reserve of great immigration potential, hence a prime target for the Zionists…"[311]

A senior Mossad commander anticipated that even these might not wish to come to Palestine and would need to be actively recruited: "We must not think that thousands upon thousands will come knocking at the country's gates once they open. The Zionist movement must understand that it must be first on the market."[312]

When only a minority of Jewish refugees wished to go to Palestine, a report by Zionist operative Rabbi Klaussner concluded, "[T]he people must be forced to go to Palestine."

Author Alfred Lilienthal reports that Zionists working in the refugee camps employed numerous means to compel residents to agree to go to Palestine, including confiscation of food rations, dismissal from work, expulsion from the camps, taking away legal protection and visa rights, and, in one case, "even the public flogging of a recalcitrant recruit for the Israel Army."[313]

The Jewish Brigade of the British Army, a unit long sought by Zionists and finally created in the final months of the war,[314] was one of the first on the scene. Its soldiers and officers turned into clandestine emissaries of the Zionist movement.[315]

Grodzinsky reports, "One role Brigade soldiers took upon themselves was to gather Jewish children hidden away in monasteries, or with non-Jewish families."[316]

He writes, "Jewish orphans were to be found in many places, having survived thanks to the goodness of

Christian families and institutions that hid them throughout the war." Now the Brigade's soldiers, directed by the Jewish Agency's Diaspora Center, were retrieving them and taking them to special orphanages, "where they were to be cared for, receive Zionist education, and be trained for immigration to Palestine."

Grodzinsky reports that the process was not always easy. "Many families who rescued Jewish children were now treating them as if they were their own. To retrieve these children, Brigade men occasionally resorted to force."

Future Israeli Major General Yossi Peled and his sisters were among them. They had been raised by a Christian family almost from infancy. Brigade soldiers "came in one day, armed, and threatened [the adoptive parents] saying that 'these are Jewish children and they must give us away, otherwise they would suffer'. They had no choice but hand us over, and we were put in a Jewish orphanage in Belgium." [317]

The children tried to refuse to leave the house, and one of his sisters later said that her brother's "screams still echo in her head."

One of the best-known orphanages, Selvino House, was run by Brigade soldiers who implemented strict rules, including requiring that only Hebrew be spoken. Children were not permitted to leave the orphanage to search for relatives out of concern that they might then stay in Europe rather than go to Palestine.

Grodzinsky goes on to report that thousands of children passed through such institutions, "their period of residence there being just another part of 'the journey to the promised land.'"[318]

In July 1945 Zionists organized the "First Congress of Jewish Survivors in Germany," which issued a proclamation calling for the "immediate establishment of a Jewish State in Palestine." While the proclamation claimed to represent the survivors, in reality most of the ten signatories were Zionist envoys from Palestine.[319]

Future Israeli Prime Minister David Ben-Gurion believed that Palestine should be the only destination for Jewish survivors.

Grodzinsky and other Israeli authors provide little-known context for the odyssey of the 4,500 survivors from German camps who set sail in July 1947 as illegal immigrants on a ship later named *Exodus*.

Baruch Kimmerling, an Israeli professor and author of nine books on the founding tenets of Zionism, writes, "The real story of the ship was far less glorious than the one told in Leon Uris's 1958 bestseller and Otto Preminger's 1960 film." Israeli author Idith Zertal calls it "an orchestrated media event."[320]

Kimmerling, citing Zertal's research, writes that Ben-Gurion "felt that the plight of Jewish refugees in Europe needed to be dramatized in order to attract more sympathy for the Jewish struggle over Palestine."

While many people have heard that British authorities refused to allow their illegal immigration into Palestine and forced the boat to be returned to Germany, few know that the French government had agreed to host the refugees. Ben-Gurion rejected this solution, and the survivors were forced, unnecessarily, to remain on board for seven months.

Kimmerling commented: "Ben-Gurion's strategy in the *Exodus* affair paid off. The fate of the refugee ship attracted considerable and sympathetic attention around the world, and served the Zionist cause well. Few observers at the time knew that many of the refugees from the *Exodus* had applied for immigration visas to the United States, and were hardly anxious to settle in Israel."

Kimmerling points out, "By dramatizing the fate of the survivors, in whom he had little interest except as future residents of the state he was building... Ben-Gurion helped to make Israel the world's chief power broker over Jewish affairs. Under his leadership, Israel established a claim to represent all of world Jewry, and on this basis successfully claimed reparations from the Federal Republic of Germany."[321]

Kimmerling and Zertal point out that this enabled Israel to acquire the right to speak not only for living Jews but also for those who had perished under the Nazis, "to whom Ben-Gurion suggested granting symbolic citizenship – in effect, turning them into martyrs for the Jewish state." This despite the fact that some, possibly many, had been anti-Zionist.

Zionists implement forced conscription

Grodzinsky reports that Zionist leaders determined that they needed to implement forced conscription if they were going to attain sufficient numbers for the war they were planning against Palestinians. Since American and European Jews would never have gone along with this, they targeted the weakest population for this compulsory draft: residents of the displaced persons camps.

After a voluntary recruitment drive netted less than 0.3 percent of the DP population, a compulsory draft was implemented.[322]

This bizarre project – in which a non-nation state imposed compulsory military service on people who had never even lived in the land for which they were required to fight – was enforced through a number of mechanisms, including publishing black lists of "draft evaders," firing them from jobs, evicting them from dwellings, withdrawing their food rations, and beating them. These tactics were also at times used on their relatives.

In one camp "a father of a *Giyus* [draft] evader Wecker was beaten up, as was the father of one who did not register; in another case an old father – Richter Aizik, was beaten because his son Moshe Richter did not register for the *Giyus*."[323]

Men and women who weren't able to evade this draft "were sometimes assigned to combat units with minimal training, and given little time to get their bearings." They were paid less than volunteers from English-speaking Western countries and had fewer privileges.[324] Many could not even understand their Hebrew orders. Some died in battle, others died unknown, as Grodzinsky reports, "having had neither a home nor a family to come back to."[325]

Israeli author Tom Segev reports that most of the immigrants from Germany were refugees who came "against their will... They were not Zionists." In Israel they were "objects of condescension and contempt."[326]

The American public, however, was led to believe that European Jews desperately wished to go to Palestine, and the well organized, well funded, and frequently ruthless operation behind the emigration was hidden from view. Funding for the emigrant-recruitment operation included $25 million from the nongovernmental organization the American Jewish Joint Distribution Committee.

A British general who had been Eisenhower's deputy and was credited with the buildup for the Normandy invasion, Sir Frederick Morgan, noticed what was going on. He publicly pointed out that many of the refugees headed for Palestine were well dressed and well fed – "their pockets bulging with money" – and concluded that something must be encouraging their emigration.

The World Jewish Congress stated officially and duplicitously, "General Morgan's allegation of a 'secret Jewish force inside Europe aiming at a mass exodus to Palestine' is… fantastically untrue."

Morgan was forced to apologize, even though, as a pro-Israel author writes, "Morgan's analysis of the situation was quite correct."[327]

The Sieff group:
Blocking a counter-Balfour declaration

Another secret group working on behalf of Zionism was formed in 1942 by Israel M. Sieff, a British clothing magnate who was temporarily living in the U.S.

The Sieff group was, as historian Peter Grose puts it, "a sophisticated version of Brandeis's Parushim."

While its existence was never openly acknowledged, it grew into the secret back channel to officials in Washington during the last years of FDR's presidency and the critical first years of Truman's.

Its members included such men as Ben Cohen, a member of the White House staff; Robert Nathan, in intelligence; David Ginsburg, a New Deal bureaucrat; David Lilienthal, chairman of the Tennessee Valley Authority; and David Niles, a high White House official under both Roosevelt and Truman. Grose reports:

"The little nucleus possessed the entree and the clout to carry the message of Jewish Palestine into the highest policymaking circles – through casual suggestion, indirection, chance remarks among well-placed colleagues in the corridors of power and the salons of social Washington."[328]

On July 27, 1943, US State Department officials and English diplomats, concerned that Zionist activities were causing serious harm to the war effort, almost issued a "reverse Balfour" declaration calling for these activities to cease. The Sieff group, Felix Frankfurter, Henry Morgenthau, Jr., David Niles, Bernard Baruch and others took emergency action and blocked the declaration.[329]

Chapter Fourteen

PALESTINIAN REFUGEES

By 1949, Israel's "War of Independence" and ethnic cleansing[330] had created hundreds of thousands of Palestinian refugees. The U.S. Representative in Israel sent an urgent report to Truman:

"Arab refugee tragedy is rapidly reaching catastrophic proportions and should be treated as a disaster...Of approximately 400,000 refugees approaching winter with cold heavy rains will, it is estimated, kill more than 100,000 old men, women and children who are shelterless and have little or no food."[331]

The number of refugees continued to grow, reaching at least three-quarters of a million, and desperate, starving Palestinians inundated neighboring Arab countries. U.S. diplomats in Cairo and Amman described a disastrous situation in which the "almost nonexistent resources" of these countries were stretched nearly to the breaking point.

The State Department reported that during the last nine months of 1948 Arab states had donated $11 million to refugee aid, stating, "This sum, in light of the very slender budgets of most of these governments, is relatively enormous."[332]

During this time, the report noted, "...the total direct relief offered...by the Israeli government to date consists of 500 cases of oranges."[333]

Meanwhile, Israel had acquired formerly Palestinian-owned properties worth at least $480 million in 1947 dollars; the equivalent of $5.2 trillion in today's dollars.[334]

Journalist and academic Anders Strindberg reports:

"In the process of 'Judaizing' Palestine, numerous convents, hospices, seminaries, and churches were either destroyed or cleared of their Christian owners and custodians. In one of the most spectacular attacks on a Christian target, on May 17, 1948, the Armenian Orthodox Patriarchate was shelled with about 100 mortar rounds—launched by Zionist forces from the already occupied monastery of the Benedictine Fathers on Mount Zion. The bombardment also damaged St. Jacob's Convent, the Archangel's Convent, and their appended churches, their two elementary and seminary schools, as well as their libraries, killing eight people and wounding 120."[335]

Truman, whose caving in to Zionist pressures had helped create the disaster, now tried to convince Israel to allow the refugees to return to their homes.[336] His main representative working on this was Mark Ethridge, former publisher of the *Louisville Courier Journal.*

Ethridge was disgusted at Israel's refusal, reporting to the State Department:

"What I can see is an abortion of justice and humanity to which I do not want to be midwife..."[337]

The State Department finally threatened to withhold $49 million of unallocated funds from an Export-Import

Bank loan to Israel if it did not allow at least 200,000 refugees to return. The U.S. coordinator on Palestine Refugee Matters, George C. McGhee, delivered the message to the Israeli ambassador and later described his response:

"The ambassador looked me straight in the eye and said, in essence, that I wouldn't get by with this move, that he would stop it... Within an hour of my return to my office I received a message from the White House that the President wished to dissociate himself from any withholding of the Ex-Im Bank loan." [338]

Edwin Wright, a State Department Middle East specialist from 1945-66, was the subject of an oral history interview many years later for the Truman Library. About this interview, he said:

"The material I gave [interviewer] Professor McKinzie was of a very controversial nature--one almost taboo in U.S. circles, inasmuch as I accused the Zionists of using political pressures and even deceit in order to get the U.S. involved in a policy of supporting a Zionist theocratic, ethnically exclusive and ambitious Jewish State. I, and my associates in the State Department, felt this was contrary to U.S. interests and we were overruled by President Truman." [339]

Chapter Fifteen

ZIONIST INFLUENCE IN THE MEDIA

As historian Richard Stevens notes, Zionists early on learned to exploit the essential nature of the American political system: that policies can be made and un-made through force of public opinion and pressure. Procuring influence in the media, both paid and unpaid, has been a key component of their success.[340]

From early on, the Zionist narrative largely dominated news coverage of the region. A study of four leading newspapers' 1917 coverage showed that editorial opinion almost universally favored the Zionist position.[341] Author Kathleen Christison notes that "editorials and news stories alike applauded Jewish enterprise, heralding a Jewish return to Palestine as 'glorious news.'" Other studies showed the same situation for the 1920s. Christison writes:

"The relatively heavy press coverage is an indicator of the extent of Zionist influence even in this early period. One scholar has estimated that, as of the mid-1920s, approximately half of all *New York Times* articles were placed by press agents, suggesting that U.S. Zionist organizations may have placed many of the articles on Zionism's Palestine endeavors."[342]

At one point when the State Department was trying to convince Israel to allow Palestinian refugees to return, Secretary of State George Marshall wrote:

"The leaders of Israel would make a grave miscalculation if they thought callous treatment of this tragic issue could pass unnoted by world opinion."[343]

Marshall underestimated the ability of Zionists to minimize the information on Palestinian refugees reaching Americans. A State Department study in March 1949 found the American public was "unaware of the Palestine refugee problem, since it has not been hammered away at by the press or radio."[344]

As author Alfred Lilienthal explained in 1953:

"The capture of the American press by Jewish nationalism was, in fact, incredibly complete. Magazines as well as newspapers, in news stories as well as editorial columns, gave primarily the Zionist views of events before, during, and after partition."[345]

When the *Saturday Evening Post* published an article by Milton Mayer that criticized Jewish nationalism (and carried two other articles giving opposing views), Zionists organized what was probably the worst attack on the *Post* in its long history.

Zionists inundated the magazine with vitriolic mail, cancelled their subscriptions, and withdrew their advertising. The *Post* learned its lesson, later refusing to publish an article that would have again exposed it to such an onslaught, even though the editor acknowledged that the rejected piece was a "good and eloquent article."[346]

This was typical in a campaign in which Zionists exploited sympathy for victimized Jews, and when this did not sufficiently skew reporting about Palestine, used financial pressure. Lilienthal writes:

"If voluntary compliance was not 'understanding' enough, there was always the matter of Jewish advertising and circulation. The threat of economic recriminations from Jewish advertisers, combined with the fact that the fatal label of 'Anti-Semite' would be pinned on any editor stepping out of line, assured fullest press cooperation."[347]

Author Christison records that from the moment partition was voted by the UN, "the press played a critical role in building a framework for thinking that would endure for decades." She writes that shortly before May 15, 1948, the scheduled beginning of the Jewish State, a total of 24 U.S., British, and Australian reporters converged on Palestine.

"Virtually all reporting was from the Jewish perspective," reports Christison. "The journals the *Nation* and the *New Republic* both showed what one scholar calls 'an overt emotional partiality' toward the Jews. No item published in either journal was sympathetic to the Arabs, and no correspondent was stationed in Arab areas of Palestine, although some reporters lived with, and sometimes fought alongside, Jewish settlers."[348]

Bookstores were inundated with books espousing the Zionist point of view to enthusiastic press reviews. Conversely, the few books published that dared to provide a different perspective were given scathing reviews, when they were reviewed at all.[349]

When Professor Millar Burrows of the Yale School of Divinity, a distinguished scholar and archaeologist, wrote

Palestine Is Our Business, the American Zionist Council distributed a publication labeling his book "an anti-Semitic opus."

In fact, Professor Burrows' life history showed the opposite. He had been one of the organizers and Vice-President of the National Committee to Combat Anti-Semitism and had long been active in the interfaith movement in New Haven.[350]

In his book Burrows wrote, "A terrible wrong has been done to the native people of [Palestine.] The blame for what has happened must be distributed among all concerned, including ourselves. Our own interests, both as Americans and as Christians, are endangered. The interests of the Jewish people also have suffered. And we can still do something about it."[351]

Burrows emphasized: "This is a question of the most immediate and vital concern to many hundreds of thousands of living people. It is an issue on which one concerned with right and wrong must take a position and try to do something."[352]

Burrows wrote that imposing a Jewish state on Palestine violated the principle of self-determination, and noted that the "right of a majority of the people of a country to choose their own government would hardly be questioned in any other instance."[353]

Burrows criticized what he termed "pro-Zionist" writing and pointed out that a "quite different view of the situation would emerge if the word 'resistance' were used" when describing Palestinian and Arab fighting in 1948.[354] He wrote that the "plan for Palestine advocated by the Arabs was a democracy with freedom of religion and complete separation of religion and the State, as in this country."[355]

Burrows also discussed religious aspects, stating: "One thing is certain. Nothing that is essentially unjust or contrary to the Spirit of Christ can be the will of God. Let him who speaks of the fulfillment of prophecy remember Jer. 22:13: 'Woe unto him that buildeth his house by unrighteousness'..."[356]

In his conclusion, Burrows stated: "All the Arab refugees who want to return to their homes must be allowed and helped to do so, and must be restored to their own villages, houses, and farms or places of business, with adequate compensation from the Government of Israel for destruction and damage."[357]

He also stated: "Homes must be found in this country or elsewhere for Jews desiring to become citizens of other countries than Israel, and their religious, civic, social, and economic rights must be guaranteed."[358]

In their onslaught against him, Zionists accused Burrows of "careless writing, disjointed reporting and extremely biased observation."[359]

Another author who described the misery of Palestinian refugees (as well as Jewish suffering in Israel), Willie Snow Ethridge, was similarly attacked by pro-Israel reviewers. When she was invited to address the Maryland Teachers Association and chose to speak on her book, *Journey to Jerusalem*, she was told she must speak on a different subject. The secretary of the association explained that so much pressure had been brought on him that he would lose his job if she didn't change to another topic.[360]

Still another was the eminent dean of Barnard College, Virginia Gildersleeve, a highly distinguished personage with impeccable credentials as a humanitarian. When she wrote that Palestinian refugees should be allowed to return to their homes, a campaign was launched against her, labeling her a Christian "anti-Semite."[361]

Gildersleeve, who had been instrumental in drafting the Preamble to the U.N. Charter and had taken a leading role in creating the U.N. Human Rights Commission, later devoted herself to working for human rights in the Middle East.[362] She testified before Congressional committees and lobbied President Truman, to no avail.[363] In her memoir, she attributed such failures to "the Zionist control of the media of communication."[364]

Chapter Sixteen

DOROTHY THOMPSON, PLAYED BY KATHARINE HEPBURN & LAUREN BACALL

America's most famous female journalist of the time also attempted valiantly, but unsuccessfully, to tell Americans about Palestinian refugees.

According to the *Encyclopaedia Britannica*, Dorothy Thompson was "one of the most famous journalists of the 20th Century."[365]

Thompson's column was in newspapers all over the country, and her radio program listened to by tens of millions of Americans. She had been married to one of America's most famous novelists, graced the cover of *Time* magazine, been profiled by America's top magazines and was so well-known that "Woman of the Year," a Hollywood movie featuring Kathryn Hepburn and Spencer Tracey and a Broadway play starring Lauren Bacall, were based on her.[366]

She had been the first journalist to be expelled by Adolph Hitler and had raised the alarm against the Nazis long ahead of most other journalists. She had originally supported Zionism, but then after the war had visited the region in person. She began to speak about Palestinian refugees, narrated a documentary about their plight[367], and condemned Jewish terrorism.

Thompson was viciously attacked in an orchestrated campaign of what she termed "career assassination and character assassination." She wrote: "It has been boundless, going into my personal life." She wrote of this organized attack:

"...when letter after letter is couched in almost identical phraseology I do not think the authors have been gifted with telepathy."[368]

She was dropped by the *New York Post*, whose editor Ted Thackrey, and his wife, Dorothy Schiff, were said by other *Post* editors to be "very close to the Irgun and Menachem Begin." Begin, the Irgunists, the Stern Gang and other Zionist organizations had, according to one commentator, "inordinate access" to the *Post's* editorial board.[369]

(Dorothy Schiff, granddaughter of financier Jacob Schiff and owner of the *Post*, later divorced Thackrey and married Rudolf Sonneborn.[370])

Thompson's mail was filled with ferocious accusations that she was "anti-Semitic" for publicizing Zionist cruelties. One such correspondent told her that her "filthy incitements to pogroms" would not be tolerated by New York's Jews.[371]

Before long, her column and radio programs, her speaking engagements, and her fame were all gone. Today, she has largely been erased from history.[372]

In the coming decades, other Americans were similarly written out of history, forced out of office, their lives and careers destroyed; history was distorted, re-written, erased; bigotry promoted, supremacy disguised, facts replaced by fraud.

Very few people know this history. The excellent books that document it are largely out of print, their facts and very existence virtually unknown to the vast majority of Americans, even those who focus on the Middle East. Instead, false theories have been promulgated, mendacious analyses promoted, chosen authors celebrated, others assigned to oblivion.

George Orwell once wrote: "Who controls the past controls the future: who controls the present controls the past."[373]

Perhaps by rediscovering the past, we'll gain control of the present, and save the future.

ENDNOTES

[1] In Israel it is typically called "the Jewish lobby," perhaps reflective of the fact that today virtually all the mainstream Jewish organizations in the U.S., both religious and secular – the ADL, Jewish Federations, Jewish Community Relations Councils, the Conference of Presidents of Major American Jewish Organizations, Jewish Studies departments, Hillels, etc – advocate for Israel. For a list see http://www.councilforthenationalinterest.org/new/lobby/

Benjamin Ginsberg, in the anthology *Jews in American Politics*, notes that the "greatest triumph of American Jewish organizations during the postwar period" was to secure recognition of the state of Israel over the objections of the U.S. State and Defense Departments and then to successfully urge the U.S. government to provide Israel with billions of dollars over the subsequent decades.

Benjamin Ginsberg, "Identity and Politics: Dilemmas of Jewish Leadership in America" in *Jews in American Politics*, ed. Louis Sandy Maisel et al. (Lanham, MD: Rowman & Littlefield, 2004), 9-10.

However, until World War II and Nazi atrocities against Jews, the majority of Jewish Americans did not support Zionism. From its beginnings in Germany, Reform Judaism had rejected Jewish nationalism, and in the U.S. the Reform movement embraced universalism. Historian Rafael Medoff writes that an 1885 proclamation specifically "denounced the concept of a Jewish return to the land of Zion."

Rafael Medoff, *Militant Zionism in America: The Rise and Impact of the Jabotinsky Movement in the United States, 1926-1948* (Alabama: University of Alabama Press, 2006), 26.

In 1897 the Central Conference of American Rabbis passed a resolution that stated, "We affirm that the object of Judaism is not political nor national, but spiritual, and addresses itself to the continuous growth of peace, justice and love in the human race, to a messianic time when all men will recognize that they form 'one great brotherhood' for the establishment of God's kingdom on earth."

Naomi Cohen, *The Americanization of Zionism, 1897-1948* (Hanover: Brandeis UP, 2003), 43.

Today's unanimity was only created after years of strenuous and sometimes secretive (see Murphy, Sanua, Schmidt, and Smith) efforts to overcome the objections of anti-Zionist Jewish individuals and organizations, and even now, J.J. Goldberg's contention, made in his informative book *Jewish Power*, may hold considerable truth: "...the broader population of American Jews...

are almost entirely unaware of the work being done in their name."

J.J. Goldberg, *Jewish Power: Inside the American Jewish Establishment* (Reading, MA: Addison-Wesley, 1996), 7.

Many people feel this is a profoundly unfortunate situation, believing, as Israel professor Yosef Grodzinsky writes: "...the State of Israel and its actions actually put world Jewry at risk."

Yosef Grodzinsky and Chris Spannos, "In the Shadow of the Holocaust," *Znet*, June 7, 2005, http://www.zcommunications.org/in-the-shadow-of-the-holocaust-by-yosef-grodzinsky.html.

[2] See, for example: Tom Stephens, "Civil Liberties After September 11," *CounterPunch*, July 11, 2003, http://www.counterpunch.org/2003/07/11/civil-liberties-after-september-11/.

"Report - A Call to Courage: Reclaiming Our Liberties Ten Years After 9/11," *American Civil Liberties Union*, September 7, 2011, https://www.aclu.org/files/assets/acalltocourage.pdf.

[3] New Jersey's population is 8,864,590.

"State&County QuickFacts: New Jersey," United States Census Bureau, accessed January 1, 2014, http://quickfacts.census.gov/qfd/states/34000.html.

Israel's population is 7,707,042 (July 2013 est). Of this, approximately 5,826,523 are Jewish citizens.

"The World Factbook: Israel," Central Intelligence Agency, accessed January 1, 2014, https://www.cia.gov/library/publications/the-world-factbook/geos/is.html.

Israel's area is 20,770 square kilometers – smaller than all but four of the states in the United States (CIA, World Factbook).

"US States (plus Washington D.C.): Area and Ranking," Enchanted Learning, accessed January 1, 2014,

http://www.enchantedlearning.com/usa/states/area.sh tml.

More on Israel's population growth:

"Population Statistics: Israeli-Palestinian Conflict," ProCon.org, September 17, 2010,

http://israelipalestinian.procon.org/view.resource.php? resourceID=636.

4   Herzl is considered the founder of political Zionism and is often referred to as "the father of Israel." His seminal book *The Jewish State* (1896) is online at http://www.gutenberg.org/ebooks/25282.

The Israeli newspaper *Ha'aretz* reports: "Herzl devoted all his time to this movement, eventually dying at the age of 44, leaving his family penniless. An article in the Israeli newspaper *Ha'aretz* reports that his daughter Pauline suffered from emotional problems from youth and eventually died of morphine addiction. His son Hans converted to Christianity in 1924, at which time he was abandoned by the Jewish community and denounced publicly. He committed suicide following his sister's death. A book about Herzl's children was written in the 1940s but was suppressed by the World Zionist Organization, which decided to bury Pauline and Hans in Bordeaux, despite their wish to be buried beside their father in Austria, "probably to avoid tarnishing Herzl's image."

Assaf Uni, "Hans Herzl's Wish Comes True - 76 Years Later," *Ha'aretz*, September 19 2006. Online at http://www.haaretz.com/print-edition/news/hans-herzl-s-wish-comes-true-76-years-later-1.197621.

According to the Jewish Virtual Library, "Herzl had failed to have his son circumcised, and the Zionist leadership, following Herzl's death, saw to it that the oversight be remedied when the boy was 15 years old." Herzl himself died at the age of 44, probably from venereal disease. See:

http://www.jewishvirtuallibrary.org/jsource/biogra phy/Herzl.html

Cantor, Norman F. *The Sacred Chain: A History of the Jews.* New York: HarperPerennial, 1995.

"THEODOR HERZL." *Kirkus Reviews.* Accessed February 19, 2014.

https://www.kirkusreviews.com/book-reviews/desmond-stewart/theodor-herzl/.

Loewenberg, Peter. *Decoding the Past: The Psychohistorical Approach.* New Brunswick, NJ, U.S.A.: Transaction Publishers, 1996.

Theodor Herzl, Artist and Politician. by Desmond Stewart, Review by: Peter Johnson, *MERIP Reports*, No. 27 (Apr., 1974), pp. 28-30.

Article Stable URL:

http://www.jstor.org/stable/3011339

5 Kathleen Christison, *Perceptions of Palestine: Their Influence on U.S. Middle East Policy,* 1st ed. (Berkeley, Calif: University of California, 2000), 22.

John Herbert Davis, *The Evasive Peace: a Study of the Zionist/Arab Problem,* 1st American ed. (New York: New World Press, 1970), 1.

It was first called the Zionist Organization; its name officially changed to the World Zionist Organization (WZO) in 1960. Most people use the two names interchangeably.

According to the WZO website, today the organization "consists of the following bodies: The World Zionist Unions, international Zionist federations; and international organizations that define themselves as Zionist, such as WIZO, Hadassah, Bnai-Brith, Maccabi, the International Sephardic Federation, the three streams of world Judaism (Orthodox, Conservative, Reform), delegation from the CIS – Commonwealth of Independent States (former Soviet Union), the World Union of Jewish Students (WUJS), and more."

"Mission Statement," World Zionist Organization, accessed January 1, 2014,

http://www.wzo.org.il/Mission-Statement.

6 John W. Mulhall, CSP, America and the Founding of Israel: an Investigation of the Morality of America's Role (Los Angeles: Deshon, 1995), 47-52.

"...the Galveston Immigration Scheme (GIS) brought 10,000 Jews to Texas between 1906 and 1914; ITO [Jewish Territorial Organization] ran GIS from

1907 until GIS ended at the start of World War I."
(Mulhall, *America*, 52)

[7] Justin McCarthy, The Population of Palestine:
Population Statistics of the Late Ottoman Period and
the Mandate (New York: Columbia UP, 1990), 37.

See table 2.18, "The Population of Palestine by
Religion, 1870 to 1946."

Walid Khalidi, "The Palestine Problem: An
Overview," *Journal of Palestine Studies* 21.1 (1991): 5-16.
Print. Online at http://www.palestine-
studies.com/enakba/history/Khalidi,%20Walid_The%
20Palestine%20Problem.pdf.

Khalidi discusses the Zionist plans and cites a
Jewish population of seven percent in 1897, but
McCarthy provides fully documented and explained
numbers that indicate a Jewish population of four
percent.

Additional resources on the pre-Israel population
are:

Salman H. Abu-Sitta, *Atlas of Palestine, 1917-1966*
(London: Palestine Land Society, 2010).

Walid Khalidi, *All That Remains: the Palestinian
Villages Occupied and Depopulated by Israel in 1948*
(Washington, D.C.: Institute for Palestine Studies,
1992).

British Mandatory Commission, A Survey of
Palestine: Prepared in December 1945 and January
1946 for the Information of the Anglo-American
Committee of Inquiry (Washington, D.C.: Institute for
Palestine Studies, 1991).

Supplement to Survey of Palestine Notes Compiled for the Information of the United Nations Special Committee on Palestine (Washington, D.C.: Institute for Palestine Studies, 1991).

8   Walid Khalidi, *From Haven to Conquest: Readings in Zionism and the Palestine Problem until 1948*, Vol. 2 (Washington D.C.: Institute for Palestine Studies, 1971), xxii.

9   Avi Shlaim, *The Iron Wall: Israel and the Arab World* (New York: W. W. Norton & Company, 2001), 3.

10 Nur Masalha, *Expulsion of the Palestinians: the Concept of "Transfer" in Zionist Political Thought, 1882-1948*, 4th ed (Washington, D.C.: Institute for Palestine Studies, 2001), 10-13.

An example of the fanaticism to be found within some segments of the movement is represented by a statement by Dr. Israel Eldad:

"Israel is the Jews land... It was never the Arabs land, even when virtually all of its inhabitants were Arab. Israel belongs to four million Russian Jews despite the fact that they were not born here. It is the land of nine million other Jews throughout the world, even if they have no present plans to live in it."

Edwin M. Wright, *The Great Zionist Cover-up: A Study and Interpretation* (Cleveland: Northeast Ohio Committee on Middle East Understanding, 1975), 1.

Wright cites the *Times of Israel*, August 19, 1969, for the quote.

Eldad was a strategist for a pre-state underground militia who later became a lecturer at several Israeli universities, authored a number of books, and in 1988, was awarded Israel's Bialik Prize for his contributions to Israeli thought.

Another example is described by Israeli Uri Avneri, who quotes a song that was being sung while he was growing up in Palestine: (cited by Wright, *Zionist Cover-up*, 9)

> "We have returned, Young and Powerful
>   We have returned, We the Mighty
> To conquer our Homeland, In a storm of War,
>   To redeem our land, with a lofty hand,
> With blood and fire, Judea fell
>   With blood and fire, Judea shall rise."

Noted Israeli scholar Benjamin Beit-Hallahmi, writes: "There are stories of how early Zionist leaders were unaware of the existence of a native population in Palestine: they thought the land was uninhabited and were shocked to discover the Arabs. It is hard to believe such stories…"

He goes on to write: "Looking at the writings of Zionist leaders and intellectuals at the turn of the century, we discover that the presence of natives was not only known but recognized immediately as both a moral issue and a practical question." Beit-Hallahmi quotes a number of such writings from the late 1800s on. He reports that the leading Hebrew periodical of its time, Hashiloah, "During the first decade of the twentieth century… published scores of articles dealing with the Arab national movement (using this exact term!)…"

Benjamin Beit-Hallahmi, *Original Sins: Reflections on the History of Zionism and Israel* (New York: Olive Branch, 1993), 72-77.

He gives several quotes demonstrating this knowledge.

11 Dr. Max Nordau was a close associate of Theodor Herzl. This statement is quoted in the *Maccabaean*, Vol. 7 (1904). (Cohen, *Americanization of Zionism*, 1)

12 Cohen, Americanization of Zionism, 1.

She continued: "Indeed, the American Jewish investment in the development and preservation of the Jewish state has continued to the present day."

According to the Jewish Women's archive, Cohen was a "prolific author and noted educator and academic [who] has achieved prominence as a historian of the United States and Jewish Americans." She was on the faculties of Hunter College of the City University of New York, the Graduate Center of the City University of New York, and of the Jewish Theological Seminary of America. Upon her retirement in 1996 she moved to Israel.

Tamar Kaplan Appel, "Naomi W. Cohen," Jewish Women's Archive, accessed January 1, 2014, http://jwa.org/encyclopedia/article/cohen-naomi-w.

13 An earlier project with both a domestic and international focus, "The Board of Delegates of American Israelites," was organized in 1861, which coalesced to block an effort by the Union during the

Civil War to prepare a constitutional amendment declaring America a Christian nation. (Goldberg, *Jewish Power*, 97)

In 1870 the group organized protest rallies around the country and lobbied Congress to take action against reported Romanian pogroms that had killed "thousands" of Jews. The chair of the Senate Foreign Relations Committee suggested that such reports might be exaggerated, but under pressure from the "Israelite" board, the Senate ordered the committee to take up the matter with the State Department. Eventually, it turned out the total killed had been zero. (Goldberg, *Jewish Power*, 98-99)

In their book on foreign lobbying in Washington, *The Power Peddlers*, authors Russell Warren Howe and Sarah Hays Trott write that the American Jewish Committee's history of Jewish lobbying on behalf of both American and foreign Jews began in the mid-nineteenth century.

Russell Warren Howe and Sarah Hays Trott, *The Power Peddlers: How Lobbyists Mold America's Foreign Policy* (Garden City, NY: Doubleday, 1977), 284.

Howe and Trott write, "The first lobby link with Palestine came in 1881, when Jewish American groups wrote to General Lewis Wallace," the author of *Ben Hur* and then U.S. minister to the Ottoman Empire (which included Palestine), to intercede on behalf of American Jews who had retired to Jerusalem and were allegedly being harassed. (Howe, *Power Peddlers*, 285)

14 Diane Lichtenstein, "Emma Lazarus," Jewish Virtual Library, accessed January 1, 2014, http://www.jewishvirtuallibrary.org/jsource/biography /lazarus.html.

Historian Jonathan Sarna calls her "the foremost advocate (to that time) of what would become known as American Zionism " aimed at "establishment of a free Jewish state."

Jonathan Sarna, *American Judaism: A History* (New Haven: Yale UP, 2004), 139-40.

15 Jonathan D. Sarna, Ellen Smith, and Scott-Martin Kosofsky, eds, *The Jews of Boston* (New Haven: Yale UP, Combined Jewish Philanthropies of Greater Boston, 2005), 252. Online at http://books.google.com/books/about/The_Jews_Of _Boston.html?id=sz5UJ1Lh21IC.

"Israel, flag of," *Encyclopaedia Britannica Online*, accessed January 1, 2014, http://www.britannica.com/EBchecked/topic/135532 2/Israel-flag-of.

16 David G. Dalin, "At the Summit: Presidents, Presidential Appointments, and Jews," in *Jews in American Politics*, ed. Louis Sandy Maisel et al. (Lanham, MD: Rowman & Littlefield, 2004), 31-32.

17 Dalin, "At the Summit," 31-32.

The appointee was Oscar Straus, whose brothers owned Macy's Department Store and whom Theodore Roosevelt later named to his cabinet. Dalin reports a humorous incident that occurred at a dinner years later for Straus and Roosevelt:

"In his remarks, Roosevelt had stated that Straus had been appointed on the basis of merit and ability alone; the fact that he was Jewish had played no part in Roosevelt's decision to appoint him. A few minutes later, in introducing Straus, [another speaker, the Jewish financier and philanthropist Jacob] Schiff, who was a bit deaf and had evidently not heard Roosevelt's remarks, recounted how Roosevelt had sought his advice as to who would be the most suitable and eminent Jewish leader to appoint to his cabinet."

The 30-year pattern ended in 1917 when Turkey broke off diplomatic relations after the U.S. declared war on Germany; after the war Turkey no longer controlled Palestine.

18 Thomas A. Kolsky, *Jews against Zionism: the American Council for Judaism, 1942-1948* (Philadelphia: Temple UP, 1990), 24.

19 Kolsky, *Jews against Zionism*, 24.

20 Kolsky, *Jews against Zionism*, 24.

In a 1918 reorganization the FAZ renamed itself the Zionist Organization of America (ZOA). (Kolsky, *Jews against Zionism*, 26)

21 Donald Neff, *Fallen Pillars: U.S. Policy towards Palestine and Israel since 1945*, Reprint ed. (Washington D.C.: Institute for Palestine Studies, 2002), 8.

22 Kolsky, *Jews against Zionism*, 25.

23 Neff, *Pillars*, 17; Edward Tivnan, *The Lobby: Jewish Political Power and American Foreign Policy* (New York: Simon and Schuster, 1987), 30.

24 Richard P. Stevens, *American Zionism and U.S. Foreign Policy 1942-1947,* Reprinted by the Institute for Palestine Studies, 1970 (New York: Pageant Press: 1962), 20.

25 Neff, *Pillars,* 9.

26 Neff, *Pillars,* 10.

27 While Brandeis' beloved uncle had been a Zionist, it appears that Brandeis himself had not become a Zionist until later in life. The main person credited with his conversion to Zionism was a journalist named Jacob De Haas. De Haas had been sent to the U.S. ten years before Brandeis met him by Zionist founder Theodor Herzl to recruit Americans to the cause.

Peter Grose, "Louis Brandeis, Arthur Balfour and a Declaration That Made History," *Moment* 8, no. 10 (November 1983): 27-28. Online at http://search.opinionarchives.com/Summary/Moment /V8I10P27-1.htm.

According to its website, *Moment Magazine* is "North America's premier Jewish magazine." It was founded in 1975 by Elie Wiesel and Leonard Fein.

28 Neff, *Pillars,* 10; Christison, *Perceptions,* 28; Robert John and Sami Hadawi, *The Palestine Diary: 1914-1945, Britain's Involvement,* Vol. 1, Reprint of Third Ed. (Charleston: BookSurge, 2006), 59.

29 Urofsky, Melvin. Louis D. Brandeis: A Life. New York, NY: Pantheon Books, 2009. 438. Urofsky, an Israel partisan and Brandeis champion, while noting that the campaign against Brandeis centered on ethical questions, attributed the motivation to political differences.

[30] Regarding the possible role of anti-Semitism in the opposition to Brandeis, it seems that his ethnicity may actually have enhanced his chances. Many Jewish leaders, while disliking his Zionism, felt they must support him. Similarly, many non-Jews, fearful of being called anti-Semitic, remained silent. Journalist Gus Karger reported at the time that "many Senators who might base their opposition to him on sound and logical grounds, if he were a Presbyterian, are reluctant to take a stand, lest their opposition be misconstrued." (Urofsky, *Brandeis,* 440)

[31] Bruce Allen Murphy, *The Brandeis/Frankfurter Connection: The Secret Political Activities of Two Supreme Court Justices* (New York: Oxford UP, 1982), 10.

Bruce Murphy is a judicial biographer and scholar of American Constitutional law and politics and is the Fred Morgan Kirby Professor of Civil Rights at Lafayette College. He holds a PhD from the University of Virginia. This book received a Certificate of Merit from the American Bar Association.

[32] Murphy, *Brandeis/Frankfurter Connection,* 10.

[33] Murphy, *Brandeis/Frankfurter Connection,* 10.

[34] Murphy, *Brandeis/Frankfurter Connection,* 44.

[35] *New York Times,* "Judging Judges, and History," editorial, February 18, 1982, Late City Final ed., Section A, http://www.nytimes.com/1982/02/18/opinion/judging-judges-and-history.html.

[36] Murphy, *Brandeis/Frankfurter Connection,* 10; back cover flap.

[37] Murphy, *Brandeis/Frankfurter Connection,* 11.

38 Michael Alexander, *Jazz Age Jews* (Princeton, NJ: Princeton UP, 2001), 83.

39 Murphy, *Brandeis/Frankfurter Connection*, 39.

40 Murphy, *Brandeis/Frankfurter Connection*, 39.

41 It is surprising how extremely buried this information remains. After I posted Sarah Schmidt's article on it (see footnote below) online in 2010 and mentioned it in my online and print drafts of this book, another book released this year mentions the society, but fails to report accurately on its covert nature and significant activities.

42 A positive review of the book in *Foreign Policy* stated: "[Grose] is not a one-sided partisan; he exposes the faults and foibles of all concerned (above all, the State Department). What slant the book has derives from his chosen theme: that America and the Jewish state are 'bonded together' through history and shared values."

   John C. Campbell, "Israel in the Mind of America," review of *Israel in the Mind of America*, by Peter Grose, *Foreign Affairs*, Spring 1984. Online at http://www.foreignaffairs.com/articles/38470/john-c-campbell/israel-in-the-mind-of-america.

43 Sarah Schmidt, "The Parushim: A Secret Episode in American Zionist History," *American Jewish Historical Quarterly* 65, Dec (1975): 121-39. Online at http://ifamericansknew.org/history/parushim.html.

   Sarah Schmidt, *Horace M. Kallen: Prophet of American Zionism* (Brooklyn, NY: Carlson, 1995), 77.

   Dr. Sarah Schmidt teaches courses related to modern Jewish history at the Rothberg International

School of the Hebrew University of Jerusalem, with an emphasis both on Israeli and American Jewish history. She is also associated with the Jerusalem Center for Public Affairs (focused on "Israeli Security, Regional Diplomacy, and International Law") See http://jcpa.org/researcher/dr-sarah-schmidt.

Peter Grose, *Israel in the Mind of America* (New York: Knopf, 1984).

"Peter Grose Papers, 1942-1999: Preliminary Finding Aid," Princeton University Library, accessed January 1, 2014, http://findingaids.princeton.edu/collections/MC227.

Peter Grose was an editor and specialist on the history of intelligence and an editor for the *New York Times* and *Foreign Affairs*. He held a position at the Belfer Center for Science and International Affairs, John F. Kennedy School of Government, Harvard University. He is the author of a number of books on modern U.S. history.

44 Peter Grose, *Israel in the Mind of America* (New York: Knopf, 1984), 53.

45 Peter Grose, "Brandeis, Balfour and a Declaration," 31.

46 Grose, *Mind of America,* 53.

The Menorah Society was also a largely a Zionist organization, and was similarly secretive about this. An essay from the time states that the Menorah Society "camouflaged its Zionism by organizing itself as a purely nonpartisan body so as to obtain a larger membership." The writer reports that "practically all the leaders and active workers in the Menorah organization are Zionists... the thing of which the Menorah boasts now...is its little list of prize conversions to Zionism."

Mark Raider, "Pioneers and Pace-Setters: Boston Jews and American Zionism," in *Jews of Boston*, ed. Jonathan Sarna, et al (New Haven: Yale UP, Combined Jewish Philanthropies of Greater Boston, 2005), 256.

47 Sarah Schmidt, "The Parushim: A Secret Episode in American Zionist History," *American Jewish Historical Quarterly* 65, Dec (1975): 121-39. Online at http://www.councilforthenationalinterest.org/news/isr aellobby/item/1217-the-parushim-a-secret-episode-in-american-zionist-history.

Schmidt writes: "The image that emerges of the Parushim is that of a secret underground guerilla force determined to influence the course of events in a quiet, anonymous way."

Schmidt gives the entire oath and response of the Parushim initiation:

"A member swearing allegiance to the Parushim felt something of the spirit of commitment to a secret military fellowship. At the initiation ceremony the head of the Order informed him:

'You are about to take a step which will bind you to a single cause for all your life. You will for one year be subject to an absolute duty whose call you will be impelled to heed at any time, in any place, and at any cost. And ever after, until our purpose shall be accomplished, you will be fellow of a brotherhood whose bond you will regard as greater than any other in your life—dearer than that of family, of school, of nation. By entering this brotherhood, you become a self-dedicated soldier in the army of Zion. Your obligation to Zion becomes your paramount obligation... It is the wish of your heart and of your own free will to join our fellowship, to share its duties, its tasks, and its necessary sacrifices.'

The initiate responded by swearing:

'Before this council, in the name of all that I hold dear and holy, I hereby vow myself, my life, my fortune, and my honor to the restoration of the Jewish nation, -to its restoration as a free and autonomous state, by its laws perfect in justice, by its life enriching and preserving the historic speech, the culture, and the ideals of the Jewish people.

To this end I dedicate myself in behalf of the Jews, my people, and in behalf of all mankind.

To this end I enroll myself in the fellowship of the Parushim. I pledge myself utterly to guard and to obey and to keep secret the laws and the labor of the fellowship, its existence and its aims. Amen.'"

Schmidt reports that Henrietta Szold, founder of Hadassah, the Women's Zionist Organization, was an early member of the Parushim.

She writes: "Brandeis ... began to assign the Parushim to carry out special 'missions' for him. In particular the Parushim were to serve as a school for leaders, and under Kallen's direction its members initially became the leading activists of the reorganized American Zionist movement."

Among those invited to be members were "Alexander Dushkin, an authority on Jewish education; Dr. I. L. Kandel, an educator then with the Carnegie Foundation and Teacher's College of Columbia University; Israel Thurman, a lawyer and 'Harvard man,' who would be used to propagandize among young lawyers; Nathan C. House, a 'Columbia man,' high school teacher, who could work out plans for training Jewish high school boys," I.J. Biskind, a doctor in Cleveland; Stephen S. Wise, prominent Reform Rabbi and leader in the Jewish Community; Oscar Straus; Alexander Sachs, a graduate student in economics at Columbia University; David Shapiro, an agricultural student at the University of California; Jesse Sampter, a writer and poetess; Elisha Friedman, President of the Collegiate Zionist League.

According to Schmidt, "The Pittsburgh Program seems to have been the last of the projects of the Parushim."

48 A. Scott Berg, *Wilson* (New York: G.P. Putnam's Sons, 2013), Chapter 6. (Accessed online, page number not available)

Berg writes that Kallen went on to a "stellar career," but mentions nothing of his Zionism and creation of a secret society. When Wilson hired Kallen, he became the college's first Jewish lecturer.

49 Sarah Schmidt, *Horace M. Kallen: Prophet of American Zionism* (Brooklyn, NY: Carlson, 1995), 77.

50 Schmidt, *Horace M. Kallen*, 77.

51 Ben Halpern, "The Americanization of Zionism, 1880-1930," in *American Zionism: Mission and Politics* by Jeffrey Gurock (New York: Routledge, 1998), 125-43. (Part of a 13 Volume series edited by Jeffrey S. Gurock published by the American Jewish Historical Society.)

52 Grose, *Mind of America*, 53.

53 Grose, *Mind of America*, 40.

Another organization that chose to work secretively was the American Jewish Committee (AJC), though this organization was largely non-Zionist in its early decades. Author Marianne R. Sanua describes its activities in her authorized biography of the organization, *Let Us Prove Strong: The American Jewish Committee, 1945-2006*.

Except where noted otherwise, the following information comes from pages 3-27.

The AJC was founded in 1906 by wealthy banker Jacob H. Schiff, who invited "fifty-seven prominent Jews across the country" to explore the creation of a body to protect Jews both at home and abroad. "On the appointed day," Sanua writes, "rabbis, businessmen, scientists, judges, ambassadors, scholars, writers, and philanthropists gathered in New York from Baltimore, Boston, Cincinnati, Chicago, Milwaukee, New Orleans, Philadelphia, Washington D.C., Richmond, and as far away as San Francisco."

Although part of the original group withdrew, fearing such an entity would reinforce gentile beliefs in powerful Jewish cabals, the others went forward and in many ways created just such an entity.

While the existence of the AJC, unlike the Parushim, was not kept hidden, many of its activities were. As a leader wrote about its earliest days, "The new body was not to engage in publicity except as an instrument for achieving objectives."

According to Sanua, the AJC desired "in general to remain as unobtrusive as possible in conducting its work, preferring to use the names and addresses of supposedly nonsectarian organizations instead of its own."

When necessary," Sanua writes, the AJC "would create the name of an essentially fictitious organization to hide the fact that American Jews were behind the effort at all."

In the 1930s and 1940s, Sanua, reports, "its agents went undercover, infiltrated meetings, and compiled a list of 50,000 offenders [alleged anti-Semites or German sympathizers] whose names were shared with the FBI…"

According to Sanua, scores of Americans were sent to jail "because of the efforts of the AJC," which, out of a total of 50,000 "offenders," raises the question of exactly who was on this list, and why.

In 1944 undercover AJC agents attended the first national convention of the America First Party, which had opposed entering European wars. The AJC charged that its presidential candidate, Gerald Smith, was anti-Semitic, a charge that Sanua says he denied, accusing the ADL and others of using the millions of dollars at their disposal to "hound innocent Christian nationalists with their Gestapo techniques." (Sanua, *Let Us Prove Strong*, 41)

The AJC successfully pushed for federal investigations into Smith, and in 1946 he was called before the House Committee on Un-American Activities. Sanua notes that the AJC had "pulled all their strings in Washington to put him there." (Sanua, *Let Us Prove Strong*, 41)

These AJC activities continued after the war, Sanua reports, and notes, "Again, secrecy and behind-the scenes work was the key. Most of the written records of these activities remain closed to the public to the present day."

While the AJC began as a non-Zionist organization and opposed the immediate creation of a Jewish state for the AJC's first few decades, its activities at times were helpful to the Zionist cause. The organization endorsed the Balfour Declaration, some members provided financial support for Jewish settlement and institutions in Palestine, and for a time AJC representatives served with Zionists in the Jewish Agency for Palestine.

Eventually, over the objections of many members, the AJC became Zionist, and in the watershed year of 1947, Sanua reports, the AJC threw its weight behind the Zionist cause, using its connections at high levels of the U.S. government, including in the White House, to help push through a UN partition plan intended to create a Jewish state in Palestine.

In October 1948, Sanua writes, the AJC's executive committee resolved to work for "financial aid from the United States – which it achieved the following year."

Marianne Sanua, *Let Us Prove Strong: The American Jewish Committee, 1945-2006* (Waltham, MA: Brandeis UP, 2007), 3-27.

According to journalists Abba A. Solomon and Norman Solomon, the AJC "adjusted to the triumph of an ideology – militant Jewish nationalism – that it did not share." The Solomons quote a January 1948 AJC position paper that described the actions of "militant Zionists," who were "then ascendant among Jews in Palestine and in the United States." The AJC warned that this group served "no less monstrosity than the idol of the State as the complete master not only over its own immediate subjects but also over every living Jewish body and soul the world over, beyond any consideration of good or evil."

According to the Solomons, such concerns "became more furtive after Israel became a nation later in 1948." By 1950 debate over Zionism was to be permissible only within the Jewish community – it was to be, in the Solomons' words, "inaudible to gentiles." Soon, the Solomons contend, even debate among Jews became "marginal, then unmentionable."

Norman Solomon and Abba A. Solomon, "The Blind Alley of J Street and Liberal American Zionism," *Huffington Post*, January 22, 2014, http://www.huffingtonpost.com/norman-solomon/the-blind-alley-of-j-stre_b_4644658.html.

54 Grose, *Mind of America*, 54.

American professor Horace Kallen was a major mover and the original founder of the Parushim.

In his book *American Zionism: Mission and Politics*, Jeffrey Gurock writes: "Brandeis conducted a vigorous search of his own for 'college men,' particularly young graduates of Harvard Law School, whom he co-opted to leadership or special assignments for the regular and emergency Zionist organizations he controlled. Among those recruited were men like Felix Frankfurter, Judge Julian Mack, Walter Lippmann, Bernard Flexner (one of the founders of the Council on Foreign Relations), Benjamin Cohen (high official under both FDR and Truman), and others who achieved national and international eminence."

Jeffery Gurock, *American Zionism: Missions and Politics* (London: Routledge, 1998), 135.

Parushim creator Kallen is known as being one of the fathers of "cultural pluralism," opposing the highly popular "melting pot" view, in which immigrants from all over the world would join together as non-hyphenated Americans. See, for example: Michael Alexander, *Jazz Age Jews* (Princeton, NJ: Princeton UP, 2001), 90.

Most Americans and new immigrants – including Jewish Americans – were opposed to Kallen's creation of cultural pluralism and hyphenated Americans, preferring assimilation and the melting pot. See, for example, Cohen, *Americanization of Zionism*, 18: "Most [Jews] had found their promised land in America." One of the primary goals in the U.S. for some Zionists leaders was, in Cohen's words, "to guard against assimilation." (Cohen, *Americanization of Zionism,* 22) "The popular melting-pot theory was antithetical to the heart of the Zionist message." (Cohen, *Americanization of Zionism,* 15)

55 Neff, *Pillars*, 12-14.

56 Neff, *Pillars*, 12; Grose, *Mind of America*, 57-58.

Brandeis also "played a decisive role in planning Wilson's economic program, and particularly in formulating the Federal Reserve."

Benjamin Ginsberg, *The Fatal Embrace: Jews and the State* (Chicago: University of Chicago, 1993), 93.

57 Neff, *Pillars*, 12; John & Hadawi, *Palestine Diary*, 59-60.

Felix Frankfurter's work on behalf of Zionism spanned many years. FDR was to appoint him to the Supreme Court in 1939, and even before this time he used his "access to the president to bring Zionist issues to his attention and urge his intercession on behalf of the Zionist cause. (Christison, *Perceptions*, 47)

"At Brandeis's behest, Frankfurter also became involved with American Zionism. In 1917 Frankfurter accompanied Ambassador Henry Morgenthau to Turkey and Egypt to see what could be done for the settlements in Palestine during the World War. Frankfurter also attended the peace conference in Paris as a representative of the American Zionist movement and as a liaison for Brandeis." (Alexander, *Jazz Age Jews*, 91)

At the request of Brandeis, financier Jacob Schiff had donated funds to have a position created for Frankfurter at Harvard early in his career. (Alexander, *Jazz Age Jews*, 83).

58 Kolsky, *Jews against Zionism*, 25, 32.

59 "Overview of World War I," Digital History, accessed January 1, 2014,

http://www.digitalhistory.uh.edu/era.cfm?eraid=12&smtid=1.

60 "Woodrow Wilson." *The White House*, accessed January 1, 2014,

http://www.whitehouse.gov/about/presidents/woodrowwilson.

61 Over 63,000 Americans died and nearly 205,000 were injured.

"Military and Civilian War Related Deaths Through the Ages," *Tom Philo*, accessed January 1, 2014, http://www.taphilo.com/history/war-deaths.shtml.

62 Wilson's Espionage and Sedition Acts resulted in the jailing 1,200 American citizens.

"Walter C. Matthey of Iowa was sentenced to a year in jail for applauding an anticonscription speech. Walter Heynacher of South Dakota was sentenced to five years in Leavenworth for telling a younger man that 'it was foolishness to send our boys over there to get killed by the thousands, all for the sake of Wall Street.'...Abraham Sugarman of Sibley County, Minnesota, was sentenced to three years in Leavenworth for arguing that the draft was unconstitutional and remarking, 'This is supposed to be a free country. Like Hell it is.'"

Bill Kauffman, *Ain't My America: the Long, Noble History of Antiwar Conservatism and Middle American Anti-imperialism* (New York: Metropolitan, 2008), 74.

One of the songs that helped recruit Americans to fight in the war, "Over There," was written by George M. Cohan, who received the Congressional Medal of Honor for it in 1940, when America was about to join another world war.

"Who's Who - George M Cohan," First World War, August 22, 2009,

http://www.firstworldwar.com/bio/cohan.htm.

63 An intriguing article speculates that Zionists might have played a role in making the Zimmerman note public. While the article is speculative, the editors called it "...an original and very plausible explanation of a major event in world history for which no previous rationale has ever seemed satisfactory."

John Cornelius, "The Balfour Declaration and the Zimmermann Note," *Washington Report on Middle East Affairs*, August-September (1997): 18-20. Print. Online at

http://www.wrmea.org/component/content/article/1 88-1997-august-september/2646-the-balfour-declaration-and-the-zimmermann-note-.html.

64 Shlaim, *The Iron Wall*, 5.

65 Mulhall, *America*, 50.

Hala Fattah, "Sultan Abdul-Hamid and the Zionist Colonization of Palestine: A Case Study," accessed January 1, 2014, http://www.lahana.org/blog/Zionist%20Colonization%20of%20Palestine.htm.

[66] Paul Rich, ed., *Iraq and Gertrude Bell's The Arab of Mesopotamia* (Lanham, MD: Lexington, 2008), 150.

[67] Mulhall, *America*, 66.

This was a sadly deft prognosis. Writing of Jerusalem in the early 1960s, the American Consul General in Jerusalem found: "I think I can safely make the general comment that in present-day Israel... the Arabs are very much of 'hewers of wood and drawers of water'" for the dominant Israelis.

Evan M. Wilson, *Jerusalem, Key to Peace* (Washington: Middle East Institute, 1970), 33.

A number of other British officials also opposed Zionism. Charles Glass writes: "The only Jewish member of the British cabinet, Edwin Samuel Montagu, the secretary of state for India, argued against issuing the Declaration. Montagu called Zionism "a mischievous political creed" and wrote that, in favouring it, "the policy of His Majesty's Government is anti-semitic." David Alexander, president of the Board of British Jews, Claude Montefiore, president of the Anglo-Jewish Association, and most Orthodox rabbis also opposed the Zionist enterprise. They insisted that they had as much right as any Christian to live and prosper in Britain, and they did not want Weizmann, however Anglophile his tastes, telling them to settle in the Judean desert or to till the orange groves of Jaffa. The other opponents of a British protectorate for the Zionists in Palestine were George Nathaniel Curzon, leader of the Lords and a member of the war cabinet, and the senior British military commanders in the Middle East, Lieutenant-General Sir Walter Congreve and General Gilbert Clayton. The generals contended that it was unnecessary to use Palestine as a route to Iraq's oil and thought that the establishment of the protectorate would waste imperial resources better deployed elsewhere."

Charles Glass, "The Mandate Years: Colonialism and the Creation of Israel," *Guardian*, May 31, 2001, http://www.theguardian.com/books/2001/may/31/lo ndonreviewofbooks/print.

[68] The BBC history of the Battle of the Somme reports that on the first day alone Britain sustained 60,000 casualties, of whom 20,000 were already dead by the end of the day; 60 percent of all officers involved had been killed. The battle went on for four and a half months.

"Battle of the Somme: 1 July - 13 November 1916," BBC History, accessed January 1, 2014, http://www.bbc.co.uk/history/worldwars/wwone/bat tle_somme.shtml.

[69] A number of authors refer to this; see the following citations.

One was William Yale in *The Near East: A Modern History* (Ann Arbor: University of Michigan Press, 1968), 266-270.

Yale, a descendant of the founder of Yale University, was an authority on the Middle East who had worked for the State Department in a number of roles in the Middle East, including as a member of the King Crane Commission, and worked for many years as a professor of history.

"Guide to the William Yale Papers, 1916-1972," *University of New Hampshire Library*, accessed on January 1, 2014,

http://www.library.unh.edu/special/index.php/william -yale.

Yale writes: "…the Zionists in England set about winning British support for Zionism. This the English Zionists successfully did by the end of 1916. It was an amazing achievement which required great skill, unfaltering energy, and determination. The methods by which the conquest of the British government was made were diverse and of necessity in some cases devious."

He writes, "The Zionists in England well understood that British leaders would have to be approached on the basis of their interests and ideas," and notes, "The means used were adapted admirably to the personal outlook and characteristics of the men to be influenced."

Some were "persuaded that Zionism was a fulfillment of Old and New Testament prophesies." Zionists also appealed to "the idealisms of many [British]," convincing them that this was a solution to anti-Semitism and could be an "atonement by Christian Europe for its long persecution of the Jews."

Some top officials had to be persuaded "that Zionism was a noble and righteous cause of significance to the welfare of the world as well as to that of the Jewish people."

Others were to be convinced that "by backing Zionism world-wide enthusiastic Jewish support for the allied cause could be assured." Yale notes that in 1916 "the Allied cause was far from bright" and quotes a Zionist leader's statements that Zionists worked to persuade British officials that "the best and perhaps the only way (which proved to be so) to induce the American President to come into the war was to secure the cooperation of Zionist Jews by promising them Palestine, and thus enlist and mobilise the hitherto unsuspectedly powerful forces of Zionist Jews in America and elsewhere in favor of the Allies on a *quid pro quo* contract basis. Thus, as will be seen, the Zionists, having carried out their part, and greatly helped to bring America in, the Balfour Declaration of 1917 was but the public confirmation of the necessarily secret 'gentlemen's' agreement of 1916…"

Yale states that once "inner circles of the British government had been captured by the Zionists," they turned their efforts to obtain French, Italian, and American acquiescence to the Zionist program.

In 1903, Zionists retained future Prime Minister Lloyd George's law firm.

For a detailed discussion of the Lusitania incident and other aspects of the U.S. entry into WWI see John Cornelius, "The Hidden History of the Balfour Declaration," *Washington Report on Middle East Affairs*, November 2005, 44-50. Print. Online at http://www.wrmea.com/component/content/article/278-2005-november/8356-special-report-the-hidden-history-of-the-balfour-declaration.html.

[70] McCarthy, *Population of Palestine*, 26.

[71] J.M.N. Jeffries, *Palestine: The Reality,* reprint ed (London: Longman, Greens, and Co, 1939), 172.

"Drafts for it travelled back and forth, within England or over the Ocean, to be scrutinized by some two score draftsmen half-cooperating, half competing with one another..."

Jeffries also reports that American Zionist leader Rabbi Stephen Wise wrote, "The Balfour Declaration was in process of making for nearly two years."

[72] Jeffries, *Palestine: The Reality*, 172. (Jeffries quotes Nahum Sokolow's *History of Zionism*)

[73] Nahum Sokolow, *History of Zionism (1600-1918) with an Introduction by the Rt. Hon. A. J. Balfour, M.P.*, vol. 2 (London: Longmans, Green and Co, 1919), 79-80. Online at https://archive.org/details/historyofzionism02sokouoft.

[74] "Balfour Declaration Author Was a Secret Jew, Says Prof," *JWeekly*, January 15, 1999, http://www.jweekly.com/article/full/9929/balfour-declaration-author-was-a-secret-jew-says-prof/.

William D. Rubinstein, "The Secret of Leopold Amery," *History Today* 49 (February 1999). Online at http://www.ifamericansknew.org/us_ints/amery.html.

According to his publisher, Macmillan, "William D. Rubinstein is Professor of Modern History at the University of Aberystwyth, UK and a Fellow of the Royal Historical Society. He has published widely on modern British history and on modern Jewish history, and was President of the Jewish Historical Society of England, 2002-2004. His works include *A History of the Jews in the English-Speaking World: Great Britain* (Palgrave Macmillan 1996), *The Myth of Rescue* (1997), and *Israel, the Jews and the West: The Fall and Rise of Antisemitism* (2008)."

"William D. Rubinstein," Macmillan.com, accessed January 1, 2014,
http://us.macmillan.com/authordetails.aspx?authorna me=williamdrubinstein.

Amery, who had kept his Jewish roots secret, worked for Zionism in a number of ways. As a pro-Israel writer Daphne Anson reports:

"As assistant military secretary to the Secretary of State for War, Amery played a pivotal role in the establishment of the Jewish Legion, consisting of three battalions of Jewish soldiers who served, under Britain's aegis, in Palestine during the First World War and were the forerunners of the IDF. 'I seem to have had my finger in the pie, not only of the Balfour Declaration, but of the genesis of the present Israeli Army', he notes proudly.

"As Dominions Secretary (1925-29) he had responsibility for the Palestine Mandate, robustly supporting the growth and development of the Yishuv – Weizman recalled Amery's 'unstinting encouragement and support' and that Amery 'realized the importance of a Jewish Palestine in the British imperial scheme of things more than anyone else. He also had much insight into the intrinsic fineness of the Zionist movement'. In 1937, shortly after testifying before the Peel Commission on the future of Palestine, Amery helped to organise a dinner in tribute to the wartime Jewish Legion at which his friend Jabotinsky was guest of honour. Amery became an increasingly vociferous critic of the British government's dilution of its commitments to the Jews of Palestine in order to appease the Arabs, and fulminated in the Commons against the notorious White Paper of 1939, which set at 75,000 the maximum number of Jews to be admitted to Palestine over the ensuing five years. 'I have rarely risen with a greater sense of indignation and shame or made a speech which I am more content to look back upon', he remembered. And he became an arch-critic of Chamberlain and Appeasement."

Daphne Anson, "The Mosque-Founder's Nephew who drafted the Balfour Declaration – Leopold Amery, the 'Secret Jew,'" *Daphne Anson blog*, November 1, 2010, http://daphneanson.blogspot.com/2010/10/mosque-founders-nephew-who-drafted.html.

[75] Grose, "Brandeis, Balfour, and a Declaration," 39.

Historian Ronald Sanders also discusses Kallen's role, writing, "...in the first half of December 1915, the Foreign Office received a memorandum that had been passed along a chain of contacts by its author Horace Kallen, a prominent American Zionist and a professor of philosophy at the University of Wisconsin." In it Kallen had written, according to Sanders, "...I am convinced that a statement on behalf of the Allies favoring Jewish rights in very country... and a very veiled suggestion concerning nationalization in Palestine would more than counterbalance German promises in the same direction..."

Sanders writes that a week later Lucien Wolf, a prominent British journalist and Jewish leader, also sent a letter to the Foreign Office promoting the idea of working to propagandize American Jews so that they would work to bring the U.S. into the war on the side of Britain. In his communication Wolf claimed: "That such a propaganda would be very useful is evidenced by the fact that in the United States the Jews number over 2,000,000 and their influence–political, commercial and social–is very considerable."

Wolf emphasized that he himself was not a Zionist, but recommended that working through the American Zionist movement would be the best way to achieve this purpose: "...in any bid for Jewish sympathies today, very serious account must be taken of the Zionist movement."

He wrote, "The Allies, of course, cannot promise to make a Jewish State of a land in which only a comparatively small minority of the inhabitants are Jews, but there is a great deal they can say which would conciliate Zionist opinion." He suggested that British statements of sympathy "with Jewish aspirations in regard to Palestine" could be decisive, concluding, "I am confident they would sweep the whole of American Jewry into enthusiastic allegiance to their cause."

Sanders points out that Wolf's statement, "coming as it did from the spokesman of the foreign policy organ of the Anglo-Jewish establishment," seemed to the Foreign Office "as official a statement of the Jewish view of the matter as they had ever received."

Sanders, a Jewish-American author who has written several books about both Israel and Jewish Americans, writes that while the general British belief about the power of Jews in America "was greatly exaggerated, it certainly was not groundless." According to Sanders, in 1915 the American Jewish community was becoming one of the most "financially gifted subgroups" in the American population and notes, "Some of the country's greatest newspapers were owned by Jews." He also describes the importance of Brandeis, "who was to be appointed to the United States Supreme Court in January 1916, just as the Foreign Office was pondering these very questions..."

Ronald Sanders, *The High Walls of Jerusalem: A History of the Balfour Declaration and the Birth of the British Mandate for Palestine* (New York: Holt, Rinehart and Winston, 1984), 323-330.

Another person is reported to have also promoted the plan that Britain should work with American Zionists, Brandeis in particular, as a way to bring America into the war on England's side. James Malcolm, an Armenian-Persian who was close to the British government, wrote about his role in this beginning in autumn of 1916 in a booklet published in 1944 by the British Museum, *Origins of the Balfour Declaration, Dr. Weizmann's Contribution.* Online at http://www.mailstar.net/malcolm.html.

Malcolm's role and others' were discussed in a July 1949 exchange of letters to the editor in The *Times* of London. One of these is online at http://www.ifamericansknew.org/download/thomson -jul49.pdf.

More information on this topic is available in "The Zionism of James A. Malcolm, Armenian Patriot," by Martin H. Halabian, a thesis submitted for a Master's degree from the Department of Near Eastern and Judaic Studies at Brandeis University in May 1962.

See also footnote 78 below.

76 For example, Grose writes, "The promise of a Jewish national home in Palestine opened the way for the partition of Palestine, and, thereby, for Israel's statehood." (Grose, "Brandeis, Balfour, and a Declaration," 39)

77 John and Hadawi, *Palestine Diary*, 72. Citation: *World Jewry*, March 1, 1935.

78 Samuel Landman, "Great Britain, the Jews and Palestine," *New Zionist* (London), 1936. Online at http://desip.igc.org/1939sLandman.htm.

Excerpts below:

"Mr. James A. Malcolm, who..... knew that Mr. Woodrow Wilson, for good and sufficient reasons, always attached the greatest possible importance to the advice of a very prominent Zionist (Mr. Justice Brandeis, of the U.S. Supreme Court) ; and was in close touch with Mr. Greenberg, Editor of the Jewish Chronicle (London) ; and knew that several important Zionist Jewish leaders had already gravitated to London from the Continent on the qui vive awaiting events ; and appreciated and realised the depth and strength of Jewish national aspirations; spontaneously took the initiative, to convince first of all Sir Mark Sykes, Under Secretary to the War Cabinet, and afterwards Monsieur Georges Picot, of the French Embassy in London, and Monsieur Goût of the Quai d'Orsay (Eastern Section), that the best and perhaps the only way (which proved so. to be) to induce the American President to come into the War was to secure the co-operation of Zionist Jews by promising them Palestine, and thus enlist and mobilise the hitherto unsuspectedly powerful forces of Zionist Jews in America and elsewhere in favour of the Allies on a quid pro quo contract basis. Thus, as will be seen, the Zionists, having carried out their part, and greatly helped to bring America in, the Balfour Declaration of 1917 was but the public confirmation of the necessarily secret 'gentleman's' agreement of 1916..."

"The Balfour Declaration, in the words of Professor H. M. V. Temperley, was 'a definite contract between the British Government and Jewry.' The main consideration given by the Jewish people (represented at the time by the leaders of the Zionist Organisation) was their help in bringing President Wilson to the aid of the Allies."

"...many wealthy and prominent international or semi-assimilated Jews in Europe and America were openly or tacitly opposed to it (Zionist movement)..."

"In Germany, the value of the bargain to the Allies, apparently, was duly and carefully noted."

"The fact that it was Jewish help that brought U.S.A. into the War on the side of the Allies has rankled ever since in German – especially Nazi – minds, and has contributed in no small measure to the prominence which anti-Semitism occupies in the Nazi programme."

[79] Landman, "Great Britain, the Jews and Palestine."

[80] Lawrence Davidson, *America's Palestine: Popular and Official Perceptions from Balfour to Israeli Statehood* (Gainesville: UP of Florida, 2001), 11-12.

Lloyd George had been retained as an attorney by Zionists in 1903. While not yet a government leader, he was already a Member of Parliament.

[81] Mulhall, *America*, 62.

[82] Frank E. Manuel, "Judge Brandeis and the Framing of the Balfour Declaration" in *From Haven to Conquest*, by

Walid Khalidi (Washington, D.C.: Institute for Palestine Studies, 1987), 165-172.

He also writes that, according to de Haas, "American Zionists were responsible for a final revision in the text of the declaration." (Manuel, "Judge Brandeis," 71)

[83] Evan M. Wilson, *Decision on Palestine: How the U.S. Came to Recognize Israel* (Stanford: Hoover Institution, Stanford University, 1979), xv.

Moshe Menuhin, scion of a distinguished Jewish family that moved to Palestine during the early days of Zionism (and father of the renowned musicians), also writes about this aspect. In addition, he states that the oft-repeated claim that the British rewarded Weizman for his "discovery of TNT" was false, quoting Weizmann's autobiography *Trial and Error*.

"For some unfathomable reason they always billed me as the inventor of TNT. It was in vain that I systematically and repeatedly denied any connection with, or interest in, TNT. No discouragement could put them off."

Moshe Menuhin, *The Decadence of Judaism in Our Time* (Beirut: Institute for Palestine Studies, 1969), 73-74.

[84] Malcolm Thomson, "The Balfour Declaration: to the editor of the Times," *The Times* (London), November 2, 1949, 5. Online at http://www.ifamericansknew.org/images/thomson-nov49.png.

He also wrote about this in a July 22, 1949 letter to the editor in *The Times*; see earlier footnote.

85 Cohen, *Americanization of Zionism*, 37.

86 Ben-Gurion, "We Look Towards America," *Jewish Observer and Middle East Review* (January 31, 1964), 14-16. Excerpted in Khalidi, *From Haven to Conquest*, 482.

87 Kolsky, *Jews against Zionism*, 12.

88 This section is taken largely from the following sources:

Henry Morgenthau and Peter Balakian, *Ambassador Morgenthau's Story* (Detroit: Wayne State UP, 2003), 370.

Grose, "Brandeis, Balfour, and a Declaration," 37.

Yale, *Near East*, 241.

Jehuda Reinharz, "His Majesty's Zionist Emissary: Chaim Weizmann's Mission to Gibraltar in 1917," *Journal of Contemporary History* 27, no. 2 (1992): 259-277. Online at http://www.jstor.org/stable/260910.

The U.S. never declared war on the Ottoman Empire and was working as a mediator in this venture.

89 Grose, "Brandeis, Balfour, and a Declaration," 37.

90 Reinharz, "His Majesty's Zionist Emissary," 263.

91 Morgenthau was not a Zionist, but he agreed to accept Frankfurter, then a 35-year-old Harvard law professor, as his traveling companion. (Historians speculate that Brandeis suggested Frankfurter.) Frankfurter then chose the rest of the entourage, almost all of whom were ardent Zionists. The British dispatched Zionist Chaim Weizmann (who was alerted to the mission by Brandeis and others) to meet with the Morgenthau mission in Gibraltar. Frankfurter and Weizmann persuaded Morgenthau not to move forward with the initiative.

Reinharz writes: "It is possible that Brandeis, unable to oppose the scheme himself, insisted on Weizmann as the most likely person able to derail the Morgenthau mission." (Reinharz, "His Majesty's Zionist Emissary," 267)

Reinharz also states: "Obviously Felix Frankfurter also reported to Louis Brandeis that it was due to Weizmann that Morgenthau's mission had failed. On 8 October 1917, Brandeis cabled to Weizmann: 'It was a great satisfaction to hear yesterday from Professor Frankfurter fully concerning your conference [at Gibraltar] and to have this further evidence of your admirable management of our affairs.'" (Reinharz, "His Majesty's Zionist Emissary," 273)

Charles Glass writes: "Wilson sent Morgenthau to Switzerland to meet Turkish representatives. But American Zionists opposed this move, as Thomas Bryson explained in *American Diplomatic Relations with the Middle East 1784-1975* (1977). It seems that the U.S. Supreme Court Justice Louis Brandeis knew the purpose of the Morgenthau mission and told Weizmann, who promptly alerted Balfour. According to Bryson, 'the two agreed that the Morgenthau mission should be scotched, for an anticipated British offensive against the Turks in Palestine would do far more to assure the future of a Jewish national home. Brandeis arranged for Felix Frankfurter' - his clerk and later a Supreme Court justice – 'to accompany Morgenthau to ascertain that the latter would not make an agreement compromising the Zionist goal. Acting through Balfour, the Zionists arranged for Morgenthau and Frankfurter to meet Dr Weizmann at Gibraltar, where he deterred Morgenthau from his task.'"

Glass, "The Mandate Years."

92 Grose, "Brandeis, Balfour, and a Declaration," 37.

93 While this subterfuge was used in the beginning years, the goal was to create a state, as Felix Frankfurter wrote: "'I need not tell you that the phrase, 'that Palestine be established as a Jewish Home' was a phrase of purposeful ambiguity." (John and Hadawi, *Palestine Diary*, 118) In the Zionists' Memorandum to the Peace Conference they stated that Palestine "shall be placed under such political, administrative and economic conditions as will ensure the establishment therein of the Jewish national home and ultimately render possible the creation of an autonomous Jewish commonwealth. (John and Hadawi, *Palestine Diary*, 125)

94 Harry Emerson Fosdick was considered to be "the most celebrated preacher of his day." One biographer called him "the most influential interpreter of religion to his generation."

"Harry Emerson Fosdick," Christianity Today, August 8, 2008,
http://www.christianitytoday.com/ch/131christians/pastorsandpreachers/fosdick.html.

Henry Sloane Coffin, a prominent theologian featured on the cover of Time magazine, was the uncle of William Sloane Coffin, one of America's most famous clergymen, "considered by some to be one of America's great moral and religious leaders."

"William Sloane Coffin," PBS.org, March 5, 2004, http://www.pbs.org/now/society/coffin.html.

William also opposed Israeli actions.

William Sloane Coffin, *The Collected Sermons of William Sloane Coffin: The Riverside Years*, Vol. 1 (Louisville, Westminster John Knox Press: 2008), 65.

95 Paul Charles Merkley, *Christian Attitudes towards the State of Israel* (Montreal: McGill-Queen's UP, 2001), 6.

"Religion: Protagonist," *Time*, November 16, 1925, http://www.time.com/time/magazine/article/0,9171,7 22722-1,00.html.

"Protestant Church Leader Warns Against Political Zionism; Says Judaism is a Religion," *Jewish Telegraphic Agency,* January 26, 1949, http://archive.jta.org/article/1949/01/26/3017334/pr otestant-church-leader-warns-against-political-zionism-says-judaism-is-a-religion.

96 Mulhall, *America*, 76-77; John and Hadawi, *Palestine Diary*, 129; Davidson, *America's Palestine*, 20.

97 Mulhall, *America*, 77. Online at http://www.al-bushra.org/America/ch5.html.

98 Mulhall, *America*, 77.

99 Sami Hadawi, *Bitter Harvest: Palestine Between 1914-1979* (New-York: Caravan, 1979), 17-18.

100 Mulhall, *America*, 79.

101 Mulhall, *America*, 78.

102 Grose, *Mind of America*, 88.

103 Mulhall, *America*, 79.

104 Norman E. Saul writes: "The widely publicized American Jewish delegation to the region followed on

the King-Crane Commission and over-shadowed it, at least in terms of press coverage. It included Chaim Weizmann, Brandeis, Frankfurter, and other prominent Jewish leaders; Crane was certainly aware of its presence but still hoped that Brandeis [who was a longtime friend and associate of Crane] would support the commission's recommendations." Brandeis's group, however, did not support the King-Crane commission and instead publicized a report that supported the Zionist position.

Norman E. Saul, The Life and Times of Charles R. Crane, 1858–1939: American Businessman, Philanthropist, and a Founder of Russian Studies in America (Lanham, MD: Lexington Books, 2012), 196.

Brandeis' trip was taken at the urging of Felix Frankfurter, concerned at what the King Crane commission might do. Melvin Urofsky writes: "...after the State Department dispatched the King Crane Commission to Palestine, Frankfurter began insisting to Brandeis that he had to go to Palestine and contain the danger.

Melvin Urofsky, *Louis D. Brandeis: A Life* (New York: Pantheon Books, 2009), 529.

In 1922 *Editor & Publisher* published the full King-Crane Commission report, including a long introduction voicing outrage at the report's suppression. The introduction began: "Facts are first. The world is askew today because facts have been concealed or perverted. If in 1918-1919, the world had seen the international situation stripped of all camouflage, with every secret treaty opened and every national condition made clear, it would have insisted upon a totally different outcome of events."

It went on to say: "Today EDITOR & PUBLISHER gives to the newspaper-makers of the world, and to the general public, as a timely and essential source-book of facts – the facts that have been most needed and least known – the full text of this long-suppressed, much-discussed King-Crane Report."

It praised the commission: "This report, in the highest sense, is a journalistic triumph. For it shows how a small group of American reporters, or investigators, took an assignment to find out the bed-rock facts upon one of the most clouded and intricate international situations in the world. They went about their task with all the canniness, caution and courage of good correspondents. Moreover, they not only fearlessly discovered the facts and clearly set them forth, but they also followed them to their conclusions."

"First publication of King-Crane report on the Near East; a suppressed official document of the United States government," *Editor & Publisher* 55, no. 27 (1922), 19. Online at
http://wwi.lib.byu.edu/index.php/Introduction_of_the_Commission_Report.

[105] Urofsky, cited in Mulhall, *America*, 80.
[106] Mulhall, *America*, 80.

107 "The Palestine Mandate," *The Avalon Project: Documents in Law, History, and Diplomacy*, accessed January 1, 2014, http://avalon.law.yale.edu/20th_century/palmanda.asp

108 Theodor Herzl, *The Jewish State,* Reprint ed. (New York: Dover Publications, 1988). Online at http://www.gutenberg.org/files/25282/25282-h/25282-h.htm

The man who is often called the father of the political Zionist movement that led to the creation of Israel was Theodor Herzl, a Jewish journalist born in Hungary. Herzl's views of Jews and anti-Semitism were seminal to this movement (Herzl, *Jewish State*, 17) and were espoused in his books and diaries. These show Herzl grappling with "the Jewish question," espousing views that alternated between negative and grandiose views of Jews.

Herzl believed that anti-Semitism resulted wherever Jews went. In *The Jewish State: Theodor Herzl*, originally published in 1946 by the American Zionist Emergency Council, Louis Lipsky writes: "[Herzl] saw the Jews in every land encircled by enemies, hostility to them growing with the increase in their numbers." (Herzl, *Jewish State*, 15) Herzl felt that the current situation of Jews, largely living in ghettos, had created an abnormal culture, writing, "If the Jews are to be transformed into men of character in a reasonable period of time, say ten or twenty years, or even forty... it cannot be done without migration." (Herzl, *Jewish State*, 36)

The book's summary of the biography by Alex Bein states: "[Herzl] admitted the substance of the anti-

Semitic accusation which linked the Jew with money; he defended the Jew as the victim of a long historic process for which the Jew was not responsible" and quotes Herzl: "The ghetto, which was not of our making, bred in us certain anti-social qualities... Our original character cannot have been other than magnificent and proud." (Herzl, *Jewish State*, 31)

Herzl wrote: "Anti-Semitism increases day by day and hour by hour among the nations; indeed, it is bound to increase, because the causes of its growth continue to exist and cannot be removed. Its remote cause is our loss of the power of assimilation during the Middle Ages; its immediate cause is our excessive production of mediocre intellects, who cannot find an outlet downwards or upwards—that is to say, no wholesome outlet in either direction. When we sink, we become a revolutionary proletariat, the subordinate officers of all revolutionary parties; and at the same time, when we rise, there rises also our terrible power of the purse." (Herzl, *Jewish State*, 91) Later in the book he writes: "If His Majesty the Sultan were to give us Palestine, we could in return undertake to regulate the whole finance of Turkey." (Herzl, *Jewish State*, 96)

Ironically, many feel that Zionism, sometimes intentionally and sometimes unintentionally, actually resulted in increased anti-Semitism. Dr. Judah Magnes, a founder of Hebrew University in Jerusalem, later wrote: "We had always thought that Zionism would diminish anti-Semitism in the world. We are witness to the opposite."

Alfred M. Lilienthal, *What Price Israel?* 50th Anniversary Ed. (Haverford, PA: Infinity.com, 2004), 41.

[109] While this "ingathering" is often construed as a "return" to the region, a number of authors provide evidence suggesting that some, perhaps most, European Jews are not descendants of the ancient Israelites, but of conversions that took place in other parts of the world, including in central Asia in the eighth century. For more information see Arthur Koestler's *The Thirteenth Tribe: The Khazar Empire and Its Heritage*, Lilienthal's *What Price Israel*, Shlomo Sand's *The Invention of the Jewish People*, and the website and books by Kevin Alan Brook: http://khazaria.com/.

[110] Lilienthal, *What Price Israel*, 146.

[111] Hugh Gibson was admitted to the Foreign Service in 1907 with the highest grades of those entering that year. One commentator called him "one of the greatest diplomatists the USA has had in two generations." ("Letter to Michael Francis Gibson," February 14, 1955. Copy on file at the Hoover Institution.)

"Hugh S. Gibson," Wikipedia, accessed January 1, 2014,
http://en.wikipedia.org/wiki/Hugh_S._Gibson#cite_note-29.

[112] Neff, *Pillars*, 19-20; Grose, *Mind of America*, 94-95.

[113] Neff, *Pillars*, 20; Grose, *Mind of America*, 94-95.

[114] Tom Segev, *The Seventh Million: The Israelis and the Holocaust* (New York: Hill and Wang, 1993), 19.

[115] This was well known in the State Department. For example, State Department Near East expert Harry N. Howard states: "...there was discussion of liberalizing American immigration laws in this period. The Zionists opposed that liberalization on the ground that this would not be a solution as far as they were concerned. They wanted a political, not necessarily a humanitarian, solution --that is, they wanted a state."

Richard D. McKinzie, "Oral History Interview with Harry N. Howard," Truman Library, Washington, D.C., June 5, 1973,

http://www.trumanlibrary.org/oralhist/howardhn.

"The Zionist movement knows that Palestine is, and will be for some time, a remittance society. They know that they can raise vast sums for Palestine by saying to donors, 'There is no other place this poor Jew can go.'" (Lilienthal, *What Price Israel*, 27)

[116] Bernard Baruch's refugee proposal in spring 1938 (opposed by Brandeis, Frankfurter, and Stephen Wise); the July 1938 Evian Conference on Refugees; the Inter-Governmental Committee on Refugees. Mulhall reports: "Thus, even after the intensification of Nazi persecution of the Jews, and with the likelihood of a major war breaking out, the Zionists forewent the possibility of other havens in favor of Palestine." (Mulhall, *America*, 102-104)

[117] "During 1943, with immigration to Palestine limited, Roosevelt made several efforts to open up many free-world nations, including America, to refugees.

However, Zionists against opposed his plans because they did not include Palestine." (Mulhall, *America*, 109)

Alfred Lilienthal also provides details on these efforts in *What Price Israel* (26-27).

[118] Early in 1947 the British government proposed a plan that would have allowed 100,000 Jews to go to Palestine over two years, and subsequent admissions depending on absorptive capacity, but the Jewish Agency spurned it because it wanted unlimited immigration. (Lilienthal, *What Price Israel*, 26)

[119] Mulhall, *America*, 109.

[120] Lilienthal, *What Price Israel*, 170-177.

[121] Mulhall, *America*, 109.

[122] Hadawi, *Bitter Harvest*, 38. Citation: The *Spectator* (London) Magazine, 22 July 1960.

[123] Hecht, Ben. *Perfidy*. New York: Messner, 1961.

[124] Various books explore these sabotage efforts: *Eichmann in Jerusalem: A Report on the Banality of Evil* by Hannah Arendt, *The Transfer Agreement: The Dramatic Story of the Pact between the Third Reich and Jewish Palestine* by Edwin Black, *Zionism in the Age of Dictators* by Lenni Brenner, *51 Documents: Zionist Collaboration with the Nazis* by Lenni Brenner, and *The Seventh Million: The Israelis and the Holocaust* by Tom Segev.

Segev describes the accusations by writer Hannah Arendt, whose book on the Eichmann trial, from her reports in the *New Yorker*, roused considerable controversy. Segev writes that Arendt stated that many Jews would have survived "had their leaders not helped the Nazis organize the concentration of Jews in the ghettos, their deportation to the east, and their transport to the death camps." (Segev, *Seventh Million*, 359)

This information is sometimes covered up in American media reports; see, for example, my article "Denying Nazi-Zionist collusion: McClatchy, the Sacramento Bee, Darrell Steinberg, and Islamophobia," *CounterPunch*, March 17, 2001. Online at http://ifamericansknew.org/media/sacbee.html.

[125] Segev, *Seventh Million*, 19. Its Yiddish name was the "Haavara" Agreement, which was also the word used in Nazi documents.

[126] "Zionists Reject Boycott." *New York Times*, August 24, 1933, P.6 sec. Accessed February 17, 2014. "Zionists Reject Boycott." *New York Times*, August 24, 1933, P.6 sec. Accessed February 17, 2014.
http://select.nytimes.com/gst/abstract.html?res=FA09 15FD39551A7A93C7AB1783D85F478385F9&scp=1 &sq=zionists+reject+boycott+of+reich&st=p.

Some Zionists favored the boycott. Chief among them was American Samuel Untermyer, who dramatically described a "holy war" being conducted against Germany in a radio address on WABC in New York, which was reported in the *New York Times*. Untermyer called for destroying Germany's export trade "on which their very existence depends."

"Text of Untermyer's Address," *New York Times*, August 7, 1933,
http://www.untermyergardens.org/pdfs/Untermyer-Hitler.pdf.

This boycott against Germany was the subject of a strange March 24, 1933 front-page article in the British newspaper, the *Daily Express*. The bellicose report was strongly sympathetic to the boycott and may have been placed by boycott leaders. The headline read, *"Judea Declares War on Germany,"* with a drop deck stating, *"JEWS OF ALL THE WORLD UNITE, BOYCOTT OF GERMAN GOODS, MASS DEMONSTRATIONS.*

The article claimed, "A strange and unforeseen sequel has emerged from the stories of German Jew-baiting.

"The whole of Israel [i.e. the Jewish population] throughout the world is uniting to declare an economic and financial war on Germany."

The article went on to proclaim:

"World Jewry has made up its mind not to rest quiescent in face of this revival of medieval Jew-baiting.

"Germany may be called on to pay a heavy price for Hitler's antagonism to the Jews. She is faced with an international boycott in commerce, finance, and industry.

"The Jewish merchant prince is leaving his counting-house, the banker his board-room, the shopkeeper his store, and the pedlar his humble barrow, to join together in what has become a holy war to combat the Hitlerite enemies of the Jew.

"Plans for concerted Jewish action are being matured in Europe and America to strike back in reprisal at Hitlerite Germany."

The article also described anti-German activities in Britain, Poland, France, and the U.S.

While such rhetorical saber-rattling was perhaps meant to frighten Germans into ridding themselves of Hitler, its end result may have been to reinforce the kind of negative views that led to his rise.

For the full text of the article see:
http://www.nizkor.org/ftp.cgi/orgs/british/daily-express/judea-declares-war.

[127] Segev, 24.

[128] Television report by Channel 5 News WMAQ Chicago, April 22, 1984, by Deborah Norville and Rich Samuels containing interview with Black following publication of his book *The Transfer Agreement*. Black was attacked widely by Zionist organizations when his book was published. Twenty-five years later, in an interview broadcast by Book TV, he discussed his close attachment to Israel, explained that he considered the transfer agreement a necessary rescue activity, and said he is now friends with a Zionist leader who had previously censored his work.
http://youtu.be/uE2hsaHAEX0

[129] Segev, *Seventh Million*, 19.

[130] WMAQ report (see above)

[131] Segev, *Seventh Million*, 30-31, 360.

Adolph Eichmann," Jewish Virtual Library, accessed January 1, 2014,
http://www.jewishvirtuallibrary.org/jsource/Holocaust/eichmann.html.

[132] Landman, *Great Britain, the Jews and Palestine.*

Landman's booklet also contained a veiled threat that without such a state, these increasingly desperate Jewish masses might attempt to "pull down the pillars of civilization" by becoming communists.

Interestingly, Theodor Herzl, in his 1896 book, had also written of a Jewish connection to communism: "When we sink, we become a revolutionary proletariat, the subordinate officers of all revolutionary parties..." (Herzl, *Jewish State*, 91)

Historian Norman F. Cantor, in his book *The Jewish Experience* (New York: HarperCollins, 1996), on page 364 reports that "Jews played a disproportionately important role in Soviet and world Communism." According to Dr. Cantor, "The Bolshevik Revolution and some of its aftermath represented, from one perspective, Jewish revenge..."

133 Lilienthal, *What Price Israel*, 151.

Lilienthal goes on to report: "Despite these warnings, Zionist gents effectively produced trouble in Iraq. Rabbi Sassoon himself was badly beaten by co-religionists."

134 Wilbur Eveland, *Ropes of Sand: America's Failure in the Middle East* (London: W.W. Norton, 1980), 48.

135 Eveland, *Ropes of Sand,* 48-49.

For more on Eveland, see Mary Barrett, "In Memoriam: A Respectful Dissenter: CIA's Wilbur Crane Eveland," *Washington Report on Middle East Affairs* March (1990), 28. Print. Online at

http://washreport.net/component/content/article/12
5/1077-in-memoriam-wilbur-crane-eveland.html.

[136] Gilad Naeim, "The Jews of Iraq," *The Link*, April/May
(1998). Print. Online at
http://www.ifamericansknew.org/history/ref-
giladi.html.

[137] Cohen, *Americanization of Zionism*, 8-9.

[138] Cohen, *Americanization of Zionism*, 8.

[139] Cohen, *Americanization of Zionism*, 9.

[140] Cohen, *Americanization of Zionism*, 83.

[141] Cohen, *Americanization of Zionism*, 9.

[142] Ben-Gurion, "We Look Towards America," in
Khalidi's *From Haven to Conquest*, 488.

[143] Ben-Gurion, "We Look Towards America," in
Khalidi's *From Haven to Conquest*, 483.

[144] Ben-Gurion, "We Look Towards America," in
Khalidi's *From Haven to Conquest*, 483.

[145] Ben-Gurion, "We Look Towards America," in
Khalidi's *From Haven to Conquest*, 484.

Quoting Eliahu Golomb, a founder of the Zionist
paramilitary group Haganah, which later became a part
of the Israel Defense Forces.

[146] "American Zionist Movement (AZM)," *Jewish Virtual
Library*, 2008,
http://www.jewishvirtuallibrary.org/jsource/judaica/ej
ud_0002_0002_0_00978.html.

[147] Neff, *Pillars*, 23.

The executive secretary of AZEC was a man named
Isaiah Kenen, who went on to found today's American
Israel Public Affairs Committee (AIPAC), rated as one

of the most powerful lobbying organization in the U.S. Grant Smith, in his book *Declassified Deceptions: the Secret History of Isaiah L. Kenen and the Rise of the American Israel Public Affairs Committee* (Washington, D.C.: Institute for Research: Middle Eastern Policy, 2007) describes Kenen's activities in detail, particularly how he worked to elude U.S. legal requirements that he register as a foreign agent.

148 Elmer Berger, *Memoirs of an Anti-Zionist Jew* (Beirut: Institute for Palestine Studies, 1978), 9.

Originally there had been two organizations, the United Palestine Appeal (the main Zionist fund-raising effort in the U.S.) and the American Jewish Joint Distribution Committee, which was dominated by non-Zionists and which raised more money. Its purpose was to "provide assistance to Jews in the countries in which they lived, hoping to facilitate their eventual integration into those societies." Berger reports, "Never at a loss for maneuver – or dissembling– however, the Zionist manager persuaded the 'big givers' that a 'united campaign' would be more efficient than the competing, double campaigns," and they managed to push through the creation of the United Jewish Appeal.

149 Christison, *Perceptions*, 73; Wilson, *Decision on Palestine*, 134.

Wilson reports that Zionists, wishing to pressure the U.S. government to support partition and end its arms embargo, raised $35 million (the equivalent of

$349 million today) in just two weeks for the United Jewish Appeal in just two weeks.

[150] Neff, *Pillars*, 23; Tivnan, *The Lobby*, 24.

[151] Tivnan, *The Lobby*, 24

[152] Neff, *Pillars*, 23.

[153] Berger, *Memoirs*, 11.

In 1947 the American Council for Judaism submitted a 27-page memorandum to the UN opposing Zionism. ACJ President Lessing J. Rosenwald railed against what he termed Zionists' "anti-Semitic racialist lie that Jews the world over were a separate, national body."

Smith, *Declassified Deceptions*, 29.

[154] Stevens, *American Zionism*, 101.

[155] Berger, *Memoirs*, 17.

[156] Berger, *Memoirs*, 22.

[157] Wright, *Zionist Cover-up*, 25.

Wright was General staff G-2 Middle East specialist, Washington, 1945-46; Bureau Near East-South Asian-African Affairs Department of State, since 1946, country specialist 1946-47, advisor U.N. affairs, 1947-50, advisor on intelligence 1950-55. He retired from the State Department in 1966.

[158] Lilienthal, *What Price Israel*, 63.

[159] Stevens, *American Zionism*, 24.

[160] Stevens, *American Zionism*, 22.

[161] Stevens, *American Zionism*, 22-23.

[162] Melvin Urofsky, *We Are One: American Jewry and Israel* (Garden City: Anchor/Doubleday, 1978), 37.

[163] Neff, *Pillars*, 23.

Herbert Hoover, "Message to the American Palestine Committee, January 17, 1932," *The American Presidency Project*,

http://www.presidency.ucsb.edu/ws/?pid=23121.

Patai, ed. "American Palestine Committee," *Encyclopaedia of Zionism and Israel*, accessed January 1, 2014,

http://www.iahushua.com/Zion/zionhol10.html.

[164] Neff, *Pillars*, 23-24.

[165] Grose, *Mind of America*, 173.

[166] Neff, *Pillars*, 23-24.

[167] Stevens, *American Zionism*, 28.

[168] Stevens, *American Zionism*, 28.

Joseph M. Canfield, *The Incredible Scofield and His Book* (Vallecito, CA: Ross House Books, 2004).

Researchers may wish to explore an interesting though speculative discussion about what might have been an earlier effort by Zionists to influence Christians. Many years before AZEC targeted Christians, an annotated version of the bible known as the Scofield Reference Bible had been published, which pushed what was a previously somewhat fringe "dispensationalist" theology calling for the Jewish "return" to Palestine.

Some analysts have raised questions about Cyrus Scofield and how and why the Oxford University Press published his book. Scofield, a Texas preacher who had been something of a shyster and criminal and had abandoned his first wife and children (when his wife then filed for divorce, the court ruled in her favor, noting that Scofield was "...not a fit person to have custody of the children"). (Canfield, *Incredible Scofield*, 113) He mysteriously became a member of an exclusive New York men's club in 1901. Biographer Joseph Canfield comments:

"The admission of Scofield to the Lotus Club, which could not have been sought by Scofield, strengthens the suspicion that has cropped up before, that someone was directing the career of C. I. Scofield." (Canfield, *Incredible Scofield*, 220)

Canfield suggests that Wall Street lawyer Samuel Untermyer, who was also a member of the Lotus Club, may have played a role in Scofield's project, writing that "Scofield's theology was most helpful in getting Fundamentalist Christians to back the international interest in one of Untermyer's pet projects – the Zionist Movement." (Canfield, *Incredible Scofield*, 219)

Professor David Lutz, in "Unjust War Theory: Christian Zionism and the Road to Jerusalem," writes: "Untermyer used Scofield, a Kansas city lawyer with no formal training in theology, to inject Zionist ideas into American Protestantism. Untermyer and other wealthy and influential Zionists whom he introduced to Scofield promoted and funded the latter's career, including travel in Europe."

David Lutz, "Unjust War Theory: Christian Zionism and the Road to Jerusalem," in *Neo-Conned! Again: Hypocrisy, Lawlessness, and the Rape of Iraq,* ed. D. Liam O'Huallachain and J. Forrest Sharpe (Vienna, VA: Light in the Darkness Publications, 2005), 127-169.

According to the Untermyer Gardens Conservancy website, Untermyer "was a partner in the law firm of Guggenheimer, Untermyer & Marshall, and was the first lawyer in America to earn a one million dollar fee on a single case. He was also an astute investor, and became extremely wealthy.

He was instrumental in the establishment of the Federal Reserve System, was an influential Democrat and a close ally of Woodrow Wilson.

The bio continues: "Samuel Untermyer was one of the most prominent Jews of his day in America. He was a prominent Zionist, and was President of the Keren Hayesod. In addition, he was the national leader of an unsuccessful movement in the early 1930's for a worldwide boycott of Germany, and called for the destruction of Hitler's regime."

"Samuel Untermyer," *Untermyer Gardens Conservancy*, accessed January 1, 2014, http://www.untermyergardens.org/samuel-untermyer.html.

Irish journalist Maidhc Ó Cathail suggests that "absent such powerful connections, it is hard to imagine 'this peer among scalawags' ever getting a contract with Oxford University Press to publish his bible."

Maidhc O Cathail, "Zionism's Un-Christian Bible," *Middle East Online*, November 25, 1999, http://www.middle-east-online.com/english/?id=35914.

[169] Donald Neff, "Christians Discriminated Against By Israel," in *Fifty Years of Israel* (Michigan: American Educational Trust, 1998).

[170] Stephen Green, Taking Sides: America's Secret Relations with a Militant Israel (Brattleboro: Amana, 1988), 20.

[171] Millar Burrows, *Palestine Is Our Business* (Philadelphia: Westminster, 1949), 116.

[172] See citation 7.

[173] Ilan Pappé, *The Ethnic Cleansing of Palestine* (Oxford: Oneworld, 2007).

Masalha Nur, *Expulsion of the Palestinians: The Concept of "Transfer" in Zionist Political Thought, 1882-1948*, 4th Ed. (Washington, DC: Inst. for Palestine Studies, 2001).

Mazin Qumsiyeh, Sharing the Land of Canaan: Human Rights and the Israeli-Palestinian Struggle (London: Pluto, 2004).

Mazin Qumsiyeh, "Palestinian Refugees Right to Return and Repatriation" in *Sharing the Land of Canaan* (London: Pluto, 2004). Online at http://ifamericansknew.org/history/ref-qumsiyeh.html.

[174] Russell Warren Howe, "Fighting the 'Soldiers of Occupation' From WWII to the Intifada," in *Seeing the Light: Personal Encounters with the Middle East and Islam*, Ed. Richard H. Curtiss and Janet McMahon (Washington, D.C.: American Educational Trust, 1997), 38-39.

Warren and his film crew were filming an interview with Begin in 1974. "The red light had come on, under the lens. Without preamble, I turned my shoulder to the camera, stared straight into Begin's eyes, and asked: 'How does it feel, in the light of all that's going on, to be the father of terrorism in the Middle East?' 'In the Middle East?' he bellowed, in his thick, cartoon accent. 'In all the world.'"

[175] McCarthy, *Population of Palestine*, 35.

[176] British Mandatory Commission, A Survey of Palestine: Prepared in December 1945 and January 1946 for the Information of the Anglo-American Committee of Inquiry (Washington, D.C.: Institute for Palestine Studies, 1991), 243-267.

This gives Jewish ownership in 1945 as approximately six percent.

A UN map showing percentages of each district can be seen at http://domino.un.org/maps/m0094.jpg.

Israeli author Baruch Kimmerling gives the landownership in 1947 as seven percent.

Robert J. Brym, review of *Zionism and Territory: The Socio-Territorial Dimensions of Zionist Politics,* by Baruch Kimmerling, *The Canadian Journal of Sociology* 11, no. 1 (1986), 80.

It is interesting to note that the Arab position was largely based on democratic principles. At a British conference on Palestine in 1946, Arabs presented a proposal "calling for the termination of the Mandate and the independence of Palestine as a unitary state, with a provisional governing council composed of seven Arabs and three Jews." (Wilson, *Decision on Palestine*, 97)

[177] "Charter of the United Nations: Chapter I, Purposes and Principles." UN News Center, accessed January 1, 2014,
http://www.un.org/en/documents/charter/chapter1.shtml.

[178] "United Nations General Assembly Resolution 181," The Avalon Project, accessed January 1, 2014, http://www.yale.edu/lawweb/avalon/un/res181.htm.

"UN Partition Plan," *BBC News*, November 29, 2001,
http://news.bbc.co.uk/2/hi/in_depth/middle_east/israel_and_the_palestinians/key_documents/1681322.stm.

For a US equivalent, see:

"UN Partition Applied To US," Palestine Remembered, September 10, 2001,
http://www.palestineremembered.com/Acre/Maps/Story581.html.

[179] Neff, *Pillars*, 41.

[180] Noam Chomsky, The Fateful Triangle: The United States, Israel and the Palestinians (Boston: South End, 1983), 161.

"In internal discussion in 1938 [David Ben-Gurion] stated that 'after we become a strong force, as a result of the creation of a state, we shall abolish partition and expand into the whole of Palestine.'"

[181] Neff, *Pillars*, 30-31.

[182] Neff, *Pillars*, 46-47.

[183] Berger, *Memoirs*, 21.

Berger writes that in a personal conversation with him, Henderson had said:

"I hope you and your associates will persevere. And my reason for wishing this is perhaps less related to what I consider American interests in the Middle East than what I fear I see on the domestic scene. The United States is a great power. Somehow it will surmount even its most foolish policy errors in the Middle East. But in the process there is a great danger of creating divisiveness and anti-Semitism among our own people. And if this danger materializes to a serious extent, we have seen in Germany and in Europe that the ability of a nation to survive the consequences is in serious question."

[184] Richard D. McKinzie, "Oral History Interview with Edwin M. Wright," *Truman Library*, Wooster, OH, July 26, 1974,

http://www.trumanlibrary.org/oralhist/wright.htm.

"Mr. Henderson was, therefore, told, 'You've got to leave the State Department or the Zionists are going to keep after us.' The State Department suggested he be sent as an ambassador to Turkey. The Zionists had a clearance process going and they said, 'No, that's too near the Middle East, we want to get him completely away from the Middle East.' The result was that they sent him as ambassador to India to get him out of the area completely."

[185] Revealed during conversation with State Department associate.

[186] Neff, *Pillars*, 46; Wilson, *Decision*, 117; Wright, *Zionist Cover-up*, 21.

[187] Green, *Taking Sides*, 20.

[188] Henry Grady, "Chapter 9," *Adventures in Diplomacy* (unpublished manuscript), (Washington D.C.: Truman Library, n.d.), 170. Online at
http://www.trumanlibrary.org/whistlestop/study_colle ctions/israel/large/documents/index.php?documentda te=0000-00-00&documentid=4-
7&studycollectionid=ROI&pagenumber=1.

Henry Francis Grady and John T. McNay, *The Memoirs of Ambassador Henry F. Grady: from the Great War to the Cold War* (Columbia, MO: University of Missouri, 2009). Online at
http://books.google.com/books?id=7BKTLX0mppo C&hl=en.

[189] Grady, *Adventures*, 166.

Benzion Netanyahu, a Zionist who travelled to the US from Palestine to propagandize Americans and father of future Israeli Prime Minister Binyamin Netanyahu, tried – unsuccessfully – to use the Cold War as a rationale for the U.S. to support Israel. Netanyahu believed that "arguments appealing to American fears of Soviet expansion" would be the best way to win over U.S. officials. He used this argument in 1947 in meetings with Loy Henderson and General Dwight Eisenhower, but found no takers, (though Eisenhower arranged for him to meet with someone else). (Medoff, *Militant Zionism*, 146)

[190] Mulhall, *America*, 130.

Robert L. Beisner, *Dean Acheson: a Life in the Cold War* (Oxford: Oxford UP, 2006), 215.

[191] Mark Perry, "Petraeus wasn't the first," *Foreign Policy*, April 2, 2010, http://mideast.foreignpolicy.com/posts/2010/04/01/petraeus_wasnt_the_first.

[192] Perry, "Petraeus wasn't the first."

The paper speculated that the eventual goal was sovereignty over "Eretz Israel," which included Transjordan and parts of Lebanon and Syria.

[193] Green, *Taking Sides*, 20.

[194] Neff, *Pillars*, 42-43.

[195] Neff, *Pillars*, 65. Citation: "Draft Memorandum by the Director of the Office of United Nations Affairs (Rusk) to the Under Secretary of State (Lovett)," Secret, Washington May 4, 1948, *FRUS 1948*, pp. 894-95.

[196] Wilson, *Decision on Palestine*, 131.

[197] History professor Lawrence Davidson writes: "It is doubtful that Clifford was committed to Zionism in any ideological way. He would later claim that his motivation, like that of his boss, was humanitarian. However, given Clifford's uncaring attitude toward the United States' diplomatic staff in the Middle East, it is hard to believe that he was much moved by high principle. More likely, his decision to back a Zionist state in Palestine, with all its violent and destabilizing consequences for millions of people, was made simply on the basis of its ability to help forward the political ambitions of the man he worked for. It was the action

of an essentially unethical lawyer. Nonetheless, success trumps all and when Truman did win the election of 1948, Clifford's career took off. He would be a much sought after political advisor for the rest of his life."

Lawrence Davidson, "Truman the Politician and the Establishment of Israel," *Journal of Palestine Studies* 39, no. 4 (2010): 28-42. Online at http://www.palestine-studies.org/journals.aspx?id=10710&jid=1&href=fulltext.

This practice of vying for Zionist support had begun earlier. Evan Wilson, in *Decision on Palestine* (44-45), writes: "During the summer of 1944, both the Republican and Democratic conventions, for the first time ever in a Presidential campaign, adopted platform planks expressing support for the Zionist position." While the State Department urged party leaders to refrain from making this a campaign issue, they were ignored. Presidential Counsel Samuel I. Rosenman told Roosevelt that Dewey was "making quite a play" about Palestine. Roosevelt eventually reciprocated, although, it appears, to a lesser degree.

[198] Neff, *Pillars*, 63. Citation: "Memorandum of Conversation by Secretary of State," Top Secret, May 12, 1948, *FRUS 1948*, pp 975-76

[199] Neff, *Pillars*, 63

[200] Neff, *Pillars*, 29.

Author John Snetsinger writes: "Truman's Palestine-Israel policy offers an extraordinary example of foreign policy conducted in line with short-range political expediency rather than long-range national goals."

John Snetsinger, *Truman, the Jewish Vote, and the Creation of Israel* (Stanford, CA: Stanford University, 1974), 140.

[201] When Franklin Delano Roosevelt, Jr., a young Congressman, warned that the Democratic Party would lose if an anti-partition plan were proposed, Forrestal responded: "I think it is about time that somebody should pay some consideration to whether we might not lose the United States."

Zionists attacked Forrestal, who had been a WWI Naval aviator, venomously, and Lilienthal recalls that Forrestal became "the favorite whipping boy of the Zionist-dominated press." (Lilienthal, *What Price Israel*, 74-75)

Zionist Walter Winchell and pro-Soviet Drew Pearson (Forrestal also opposed Stalin) launched vicious personal attacks. (Lilienthal, *What Price Israel*, 75) At odds with Truman on a number of issues, in 1949 Forrestal was hospitalized in the National Naval Medical Center with a diagnosis of severe depression, where it was reported that he committed suicide. His brother, a businessman, did not believe this cause of death. Some question this conclusion, including David Martin whose online report contains a great deal of evidence that brings the "suicide" version into question:

David Martin, "Who Killed James Forrestal?" DC Dave, accessed January 1, 2014, http://www.dcdave.com/article4/021110.html.

Longtime British journalist and author Alan Hart's book, *Zionism The Real Enemy of the Jews, Volume One, The False Messiah*, contains probably the best information on Forrestal and his activities to try to move the question of Palestine out of domestic politics. In his chapter, "Forrestal's 'Suicide'," Hart details Forrestal's attempt to convince both Democratic and Republican political leaders to desist from promoting Zionism as an electoral tool, only to be told by both that this was impossible.

[202] Lilienthal, *What Price Israel*, 60.

Central Intelligence Agency, "The Consequences of the Partition of Palestine," *ORE* 55, November 28, 1947. Online at http://www.foia.cia.gov/sites/default/files/document_conversions/89801/DOC_0000256628.pdf.

Thomas W. Lippman, "The View from 1947: The CIA and the Partition of Palestine," *Middle East Journal* 61, no. 1 (2007): 17-28.

While today some people believe that the oil considerations are behind US support for Israel, the reality is the opposite. American diplomatic, military, and intelligence experts often warned that any US support for Zionism would endanger American access to Middle East oil. For example, Evan Wilson writes that a State Department memo to FDR that pro-Zionist statements "had given rise to a 'wave of shocked disillusionment and protest' in the Near East and that this trend, if continued, would seriously prejudice the government's ability to protect American interests, including the important oil interest in Saudi Arabia." (Wilson, *Decision on Palestine*, 45)

203 Neff, *Pillars*, 57-58.

204 George W. Ball and Douglas B. Ball, *The Passionate Attachment: America's Involvement with Israel, 1947 to the Present* (New York: W.W. Norton, 1992), 22.

Some examples:

Edwin M. Wright, a State Department expert on the Middle East who was assisting the U.N./U.S. delegation as a staff member, reports that Eleanor Roosevelt, who was on the U.N. delegation, received a letter telling her that Wright was "anti-Semitic and in Arab pay." (Wright, *Zionist Cover-Up*, 43)

"Rabbi Stephen Wise, the pre-eminent spokesman for American Zionism, and his daughter Justine Polier, were personal friends of Franklin and Eleanor Roosevelt with as much access to the White House as anyone."

William vanden Heuvel, "America, Franklin D. Roosevelt and the Holocaust" (keynote address given at the Annual Franklin & Eleanor Roosevelt Distinguished Lecture, Roosevelt University, Chicago, Illinois, 1996). Online at
http://newdeal.feri.org/feri/wvh.htm.

Eleanor Roosevelt, convinced by Zionists of their cause, had strongly opposed Loy Henderson. (Lilienthal, *What Price Israel*, 62)

When Henderson had warned, accurately, that partition would provoke violence, Eleanor responded:

"Come now, come, Mr. Henderson, I think you're exaggerating the dangers. You are too pessimistic... I'm confident that when a Jewish state is once set up, the Arabs will see the light; they will quiet down; and Palestine will no longer be a problem." (Neff, *Pillars*, 64) (Wilson, *Decision on Palestine,* 116)

There is no evidence that Eleanor ever acknowledged her error.

[205] Ball, *Passionate Attachment,* 22.

Kermit Roosevelt, "The Partition of Palestine: A Lesson in Pressure Politics," *The Middle East Journal* II, no.1 (1948): 13-16. Excerpted in Khalidi, *Haven to Conquest,* 727-729.

[206] Neff, *Pillars,* 50.

Evan Wilson notes that Truman biographer Robert J. Donovan remarked that Truman was "tormented" on the issue of Palestine, noting that this was "an exception to his habit of making quick decisions." Wilson writes that on both Truman's decision to support partition and his decision to recognize the new state of Israel immediately upon its announcement, "Truman was greatly influenced by his pro-Zionist advisers in the White House, whose advice was admittedly based on domestic political considerations. Chief among their argument was the need for Jewish support to get Truman elected in 1948, in the face of widespread doubt as to his prospects (a Newsweek poll of fifty Washington correspondents shortly before the election showed that not one of them believed Truman would win)." (Wilson, *Decision,* 148)

Wilson writes: "I began this study with the opinion, which I had held since my days on the Palestine desk, that Truman's principal motivation had been humanitarian, but after examining all the evidence, including data that were not available to us in the State Department at the time, I have been forced reluctantly to the conclusion that on certain key occasions (October 1947 and May 1948) he was more influenced by domestic political considerations than by humanitarian ideals." (Wilson, *Decision*, 149)

Former career Foreign Service Officer Richard Curtiss also describes the circumstances of Truman's decisions in "Two Politically Motivated Decisions: Truman Adviser Recalls May 14, 1948 US Decision to Recognize Israel," *Washington Report on Middle East Affairs*, May/June 1991, 17. Online at http://www.wrmea.org/wrmea-archives/131-washington-report-archives-1988-1993/may-june-1991/1634-truman-adviser-recalls-may-141948-us-decision-to-recognize-israel.html.

[207] Gore Vidal wrote: "Sometime in the late 1950s, that world-class gossip and occasional historian, John F. Kennedy, told me how, in 1948, Harry S. Truman had been pretty much abandoned by everyone when he came to run for president. Then an American Zionist brought him two million dollars in cash, in a suitcase, aboard his whistle-stop campaign train. 'That's why our recognition of Israel was rushed through so fast.'"

Gore Vidal, foreword to *Jewish History, Jewish Religion: the Weight of Three Thousand Years* by Israel Shahak

(London: Pluto, 1997), vii-viii. Online at: http://www.ifamericansknew.org/cur_sit/shahak.html #vidal.

Abraham Feinberg, in his Truman Library oral history interview, describes arranging for money to be delivered to Truman during his train campaign around the nation:

"I had already got the commitments for the $100,000 from people around the country, all of whom understood that without Truman, Israel would have had very difficult days and times trying to even come into existence. As that train went into towns where there were Jewish communities, I arranged that a Jewish delegation would ask to see the President and be received on the train and that, in as many cases as possible, they would bring him donations above these original commitments. So, the trip was a triumphant trip from his point of view as a politician... He often said, 'If not for my friend Abe, I couldn't have made the trip and I wouldn't have been elected.'"

Richard D. McKinzie, "Abraham Feinberg Oral History Interview" Truman Library, New York, NY, August 23, 1973,

http://www.trumanlibrary.org/oralhist/feinberg.htm.

[208] "Abraham Feinberg's FBI File," Israel Lobby Archive, accessed January 1, 2014,

http://www.irmep.org/ila/feinberg/.

[209] McKinzie, "Abraham Feinberg Oral History Interview."

[210] Grant Smith, *Declassified Deceptions*, 34-37.

"The Israel Lobby Archive," Institute for Research: Middle Eastern Policy, accessed January 1, 2014, http://irmep.org/ILA/default.asp.

"This weapons smuggling and other Zionist preparations for war were well-known to British and American analysts, who knew from the beginning that the Arabs would be certain losers in a war with Zionists, whose well-trained and armed combatants would outnumber the Arabs' similar combatants by at least four to one. Analysts were also aware that the Zionists planned to expand beyond the partition allotment." (Ball, *Passionate Attachment*, 24)

211 Lilienthal, *What Price Israel*, 71-72.

Snetsinger provides a number of details on Niles' close relationship with Zionists and quotes his memos on their behalf. (Snetsinger, *Truman, the Jewish Vote*, 35-37)

212 Mulhall, *America*, 127.

213 Lilienthal, *What Price Israel*, 72-73.

Stephen Green describes a May 1948 investigation into "someone in the Pentagon" who was making files available to the pre-Israeli military known as the Haganah. Evidence pointed to Lt. Col. Elliot A. Niles. "According to the agent report on the investigation," Green writes, "Niles was 'an ardent Zionist, formerly a high official of the B'nai B'rith, and lately in charge of veterans liaison for the Veterans Administration.'" Investigators concluded that Niles and another person had photostated files and sent them to the Haganah. "This particular report" Green writes, "was adjudged by its author to be rated A-2, i.e., A for 'source completely reliable,' and 2 for 'information probably true.'" (Green, *Taking Sides*, 53-54)

214 Lilienthal, *What Price Israel*, 72.

215 Christison, *Perceptions*, 69; Lilienthal, *Zionist Connection II*, 87-90.

216 Wright, *Zionist Cover-up*, 11-12.

Wright reports that "all the Near East-Africa most secret documents had been routed to Sam Rosenman."

217 Wilson, *Decision on Palestine*, 149.

Wilson served in the U.S. Foreign Service from 1937-67, many of those years involved with Palestine. Upon retirement he was given the Department of State's Superior Honor Award.

218 Wilson, *Decision on Palestine*, 98.

219 Neff, *Pillars*, 96.

220 Zionists were originally not certain that the U.S. delegation would back the proposal, historian Charles Smith reports, so David Niles worked to have Truman appoint a pro-Zionist to the delegation "to offset the views of the appointees from the State Department." Smith, Charles D. *Palestine and the Arab-Israeli Conflict.* New York: St. Martin's, 1996

221 Lilienthal, *What Price Israel*, 47. Citation: Emanuel Newmann, in *American Zionist*, February 5, 1953.

222 Wilson, *Decision on Palestine*, 125-127; Mulhall, *America*, 140-145; Hadawi, *Bitter Harvest*, 72-73; Stevens, *American Zionism*, 178-182; Lilienthal, *Zionist Connection II*, 65-69.

223 Lilienthal, *What Price Israel*, 47-49.

224 Zionist pressure against UN member countries is also described in Sir Muhammad Zafrulla Khan's "Thanksgiving Day at Lake Success, November 27, 1947" in *Palestine in the U.N.O.* (Karachi: The Pakistan Institute of International Affairs), 6-23. Reprinted in Khalidi, *Haven to Conquest*, 709-722.

225 "United Nations General Assembly Resolution 181."

226 International jurist Henry Cattan, in his 1988 book *The Palestine Question*, writes that the resolution was "vitiated by several gross irregularities."

(1) First, he points out that the UN General Assembly did not have the authority to partition Palestine.

He writes: "The UN possessed no sovereignty over Palestine, nor the power to deprive the people of Palestine of their right of independence. Hence, the UN resolution for the partition of Palestine possesses no value, in law or in fact, as acknowledged by a number of leading jurists."

Cattan quotes Pitman B. Potter's article in the *American Journal of International Law* (vol. 42, 1948 p. 860): "The United Nations has no right to dictate a solution in Palestine unless a basis for such authority can be worked out such has not been done this far." Potter goes on to point out that Arabs denied the binding force of the Mandate and the Balfour Declaration, and says "they are probably quite correct juridically."

Cattan also quotes Professor Quincy Wright's 1968 address to the Association of the Bar of the City of

New York: "The legality of the General Assembly's recommendation for partition of Palestine was doubtful."

He also cites the statement by Professor I. Brownie in his 1966 book *Principles of International Law*: "It is doubtful if the United Nations 'has a capacity to convey title', inter alia because the Organization cannot assume the role of territorial sovereign... Thus the resolution of 1947 containing a Partition plan for Palestine was probably ultra vires [outside the competence of the United Nations], and, if it was not, was no binding on member states in any case."

Cattan concludes: "It follows, therefore, that the partition resolution was not legally effective or binding on the Palestinian people."

(2) Denial of justice. A second irregularity was that the General Assembly refused to refer questions of its competence on this matter to the International Court of Justice for an advisory opinion.

Cattan writes: "P.B. Potter has observed that the rejection of the Arab requests to refer the question of UN jurisdiction over the Palestine situation to the International Court of Justice 'tends to confirm the avoidance of international law' in this regard."

Cattan concludes: "Such avoidance of international law constituted a denial of justice which deprived the partition resolution of any juridical value."

(3) Cattan points out that the resolution violated Article 22 of the Covenant of the League of Nations,

"which previously recognized the independence of the people of Palestine..."

(4) The resolution was also a "violation of the Charter of the UN and the principle of self-determination of the people of Palestine."

(5) It violated "the most elementary democratic principles by the flagrant disregard of the will of the majority of the original inhabitants who opposed partition of their homeland."

(6) He points out the "undue influence" of the US president (and others) in passing the resolution

(7) He discusses the "iniquity of the plan of partition." pointing out that "the partition plan attributed to the Jews – who constituted less than one-third of the population, who were largely foreigners and who owned less than 6 percent of the land – an area almost ten times greater than what they owned..."

Cattan concludes, "This was not partition, but a spoliation."

See also Jeremy Hammond, "The Myth of the U.N. Creation of Israel," October 26, 2010,
http://www.jeremyrhammond.com/documents/myth-un-creation-israel.pdf.

[227] Mazin Qumsiyeh, "Palestinian Refugees Right to Return and Repatriation," from *Sharing the Land of Canaan.*

Dr. Benny Morris, an Israeli historian, reports that 400,000 Palestinians fled between November 29, 1947 and June 1, 1948. (Mulhall, *America*, 155)

[228] The Arab armies were from Lebanon, Syria, Iraq, Transjordan, and Egypt. There were also a small number of combatants from Saudi Arabia and the Sudan who entered the war later.

While the popular belief is that Zionists/Israelis were fighting against a vastly larger force, this is yet another myth that proves to be false upon close examination. Stephen Green, in provides a detailed examination of the comparative numbers of forces, the reports on the situation by US and British military, intelligence, and diplomatic experts at the time, and how the myth was created. (Green, *Taking Sides*, 65-75)

See also: "Why did seven well equipped Arab armies attempt to destroy the poorly armed and newly founded 'Jewish State'?" Palestine Remembered, August 16, 2001,
http://www.palestineremembered.com/Acre/Palestine -Remembered/Story457.html.

[229] Kati Marton, *A Death in Jerusalem*, (New York: Arcade, 1996), 80.

[230] Marton, *A Death in Jerusalem*, 144.

"The Assassination of Count Bernadotte," Jewish Virtual Library, accessed January 1, 2014, http://www.jewishvirtuallibrary.org/jsource/History/f olke.html.

[231] Mike Berry and Greg Philo, *Israel and Palestine*, 36.

[232] Al Abbasiyya (4 May '48), Abu Shusha (14 May '48), Ayn az Zaytun (2 May '48), Balad ash Sheikh (25 April '48), Bayt Daras (11 May '48), Beer Sheba (21 Oct '48), Burayr (12 May '48), Al Dawayima (29 Oct '48), Deir

Yassin (9 April '48), Eilaboun (29 Oct '48), Haifa (21 April '48), Hawsha (15 April '48), Husayniyya (21 April '48), Ijzim (24 July '48), Isdud (28 Oct '48), Jish (29 Oct '48), Al Kabri (21 May '48), Al Khisas (18 Dec '48), Khubbayza (12 May '48), Lydda (10 July '48), Majd al Kurum (29 October '48), Mannsurat al Khayt (18 Jan '48), Khirbet, Nasir ad Din (12 April '48), Qazaza (9 July '48), Qisarya (15 Feb '48), Sa'sa (30 Oct '48), Safsaf (29 Oct '48), Saliha (30 Oct '48), Arab al Samniyya (30 Oct '48), Al Tantoura (21 May '48), Al Tira (16 July '48), Al Wa'ra al-Sawda (18 April '48), Wadi 'Ara (27 Feb '48).

Qumsiyeh, "Palestinian Refugees Right to Return and Repatriation."

As the carnage that the State Department had predicted erupted, Truman, belatedly, proposed a temporary UN trusteeship of Palestine to take effect after the British left. Truman wrote, "If the U.N. agrees to trusteeship, peaceful settlement is yet possible; without it open warfare is just over the horizon."

Zionists, however, mounted a campaign against "abandoning" the partition plan. This campaign pervaded both radio and newspaper news and spanned the political spectrum, from the main political parties to Communist and left-wing labor leaders, who organized a protest rally in New York attended by 10,000. Truman came under such overwhelming political pressure that he overruled the State Department and decided, somewhat secretly, to recognize the new state immediately upon its forthcoming announcement, making the U.S. the first country to officially recognize Israel. (The Soviets were the first to give it *de jure* recognition.)

The American delegation at the UN, which had been urging trusteeship, was so outraged at Truman's sudden reversal that Dean Rusk was sent to prevent them from resigning en masse. (Lilienthal, *Zionist Connection II*, 79-80, 87)

"United States Proposal for Temporary United Nations Trusteeship for Palestine," Statement by President Truman, March 25, 1948, http://unispal.un.org/UNISPAL.NSF/0/C3AFF48D7 11D26158525715400730A30.

[233] Christison, *Perceptions*, 81.

"America's diplomats… knew from the beginning that the Arabs were certain losers in their war with Israel. Every source confirmed the overwhelming military superiority of the Israelis over their Arab opponents." He goes on to give specific details. (Ball, *Passionate Attachment*, 24)

Numerous other histories of this period also report on this. See Stephen Green, *Taking Sides*, 47-75, for a discussion of troop strengths, armaments, and Zionist efforts, largely successful, to distort the facts on these in the press and in various books, including *O Jerusalem*, by Larry Collins and Dominique Lapierre, still widely marketed.

[234] Masalha, *Expulsion of the Palestinians*, 175.

There are numerous excellent books on this period. Three of the finest are: Sami Hadawi's *Bitter Harvest:*

Palestine 1914-1979, Nur Masalha's *Expulsion of the Palestinians: The Concept of "Transfer" in Zionist Political Thought, 1882-1948*, and Ilan Pappe's *The Ethnic Cleansing of Palestine.*

While Israeli propaganda maintained that the refugees had left "voluntarily," and had been ordered to leave by Arab leaders, this was refuted by both the refugees themselves and by journalist Erskine Childers. Childers examined all radio broadcasts from the time and found that none had called for Palestinians to leave; in fact leaders had often urged people to stay in Palestine. He also refuted other Zionist allegations concerning the refugees; see Erskine Childers, "The Other Exodus," *Spectator*, May 12, 1961, 672-75. Print. Online at http://www.users.cloud9.net/~recross/israel-watch/ErskinChilders.html.

[235] After the Zionist conquest of Palestine, a Palestinian man who was 100 years old described the uniqueness of its rule over Palestine: "I remember the Turks and the English. But no ruler has behaved in the way that you do. In your eyes nothing which belongs to others is sacred."

Felicia Langer, *An Age of Stone* (London: Quartet, 1988), 8.

[236] Segev, *Seventh Million*, 63.

[237] Violence between Zionists and Palestinians began in the 1920s, with both sides at times killing civilians. Palestinian uprisings against Zionist colonialism occurred in 1920 and 1929, and against the British in

1936. (Pappe, *Ethnic Cleansing*, 14) Zionists created the Haganah in 1920 (Pappe, *Ethnic Cleansing*, 16); the Irgun Zvai Leumi was founded in 1931, split off from the Haganah; the Stern Gang was founded in 1940. (Pappe, *Ethnic Cleansing*, 45) Betar, a youth movement was founded by Ze'ev Jabotinsky in 1923 in Europe, with training camps dotted about Europe. (Bell, *Terror out of Zion*, 19) Historian J. Bowyer Bell reports that members who went to Palestine foresaw "Zion redeemed through a blood sacrifice." In the 1930s the Irgun perpetrated a number of attacks on Palestinian civilians. (Bell, *Terror out of Zion*, 20-21)

Pappe writes that the 1936 Arab revolt gave the Haganah a chance to practice military tactics "mostly in the form of retaliatory operations against such targets as roadside snipers for thieves taking goods from a kibbutz. The main objective, however, seems to have been to intimidate Palestinian communities who happened to live in proximity to Jewish settlements." (Pappe, *Ethnic Cleansing*, 16)

[238] Neff, *Pillars*, 68.

[239] Mulhall, *America*, 153.

Albert Einstein, Hannah Arendt, and a number of others wrote a letter to the *New York Times* condemning this and other actions by Begin and his group. The letter, which was published December 4, 1948, provides considerable information on the situation.

Hannah Arendt, Albert Einstein, et al, "New Palestine Party," *New York Times*, Letters to the editor, December 4, 1948. Online at

http://www.globalwebpost.com/farooqm/study_res/e
instein/nyt_orig.html.

240 Ball, *Passionate Attachment*, 28-29. George Ball (who had
been undersecretary of state under Johnson and
Kennedy, and ambassador to the United Nations)
writes that the Red Cross representative Jacques de
Reynier found that 150 of the bodies had been thrown
into a cistern.

Reynier later wrote a book on his experiences (*1948
à Jérusalem*), but for many years this was out of print and
has never been translated into English. It was recently
reissued in French.

For a review, see
http://www.persee.fr/web/revues/home/prescript/ar
ticle/polit_0032-
342x_2003_num_68_2_1219_t1_0446_0000_2.

241 Ball, Passionate Attachment, 28-29.

242 Daniel McGowan, "A Jewish Eye-Witness: An
interview with Meir Pa'il," in *Remembering Deir Yassin: the
Future of Israel and Palestine* by Daniel McGowan and
Marc Ellis (New York: Olive Branch, 1998), 40.

Israeli military historian Colonel Meir Pa'il, who was
then a member of the Haganah, was at Deir Yassin
acting as a communications officer and witnessed parts
of the massacre.

243 Larry Collins and Dominique Lapierre, *O Jerusalem*
(New York: Simon and Schuster, 1972), 278.

244 Mulhall, *America*, 153; Salim Tamari, *Jerusalem 1948: The
Arab Neighbourhoods and Their Fate in the War* (Jerusalem:

Institute of Jerusalem Studies: Center for Jerusalem Studies, 2002), 96-100.

See also Sheila Cassidy, "Assault and Massacre," in *Remembering Deir Yassin: the Future of Israel and Palestine* by Daniel McGowan and Marc Ellis (New York: Olive Branch, 1998), 47-49.

Pat McDonnel Twair, "The Surviving Children of Deir Yassin," in *Remembering Deir Yassin: the Future of Israel and Palestine* by Daniel McGowan and Marc Ellis (New York: Olive Branch, 1998), 50-51.

Survivor testimonies can also be read at the Deir Yassin Remembered website.

e.g.: Ms. Haleem Eid stated: "A man [shot] a bullet into the neck of my sister Salhiyeh who was nine months pregnant. Then he cut her stomach open with a butcher's knife."

"Survivors' accounts," Deir Yassin Remembered, accessed January 1, 2014,

http://www.deiryassin.org/survivors.html.

[245] Menachem Begin, who became prime minister in 1977, was head of the Irgun; Yitzhak Shamir, who was elected Prime Minister in 1983, was a head of the Stern Gang. Neither was at Deir Yassin personally. The attack was coordinated ahead of time with the Haganah, which thereby broke an agreement that had been made with the mayor of Deir Yassin in which both sides had agreed that neither would fire against the other. The Haganah's Palmach unit took part in the attack, but reportedly left before the worst of the massacre.

McGowan, "A Jewish Eye-Witness: An interview with Meir Pa'il," 35-46.

[246] Ball, *Passionate Attachment*, 29.

Author Kathleen Christison notes that when Begin became Prime Minister, for the U.S. media "it became generally unacceptable to use the word [terrorist] with respect to either Begin or his successor Yitzhak Shamir, whose pre-state underground organization, the Stern Gang, had also committed acts of terrorism." (Christison, *Perceptions*, 172)

Shamir had approved the pre-Israel assassination of UN mediator Folke Bernadotte, a Swedish Count who had helped rescue thousands of Jews from the Nazis. He had also ordered the assassination of a top British official, Lord Moyne. (Marton, *A Death in Jerusalem*, 94)

In 1991 some of the assassins regaled the audience of a live TV broadcast with details about how they cut down the United Nations' first Middle East mediator. Shamir is the longest-serving prime minister of Israel and "frequently stated that his time as Lehi commander was the best time of his life." (Marton, *A Death in Jerusalem*, 257-258) His adopted name "Shamir" in Hebrew "means either a particularly hard rock or, according to legend, a tiny worm that broke up rocks for the construction of the Temple." (Marton, *A Death in Jerusalem*, 102)

[247] Neff, *Pillars*, 40.

On July 22, 1947, the Irgun, apparently in contact with the Haganah, bombed the King David Hotel in Jerusalem. A portion of the hotel was occupied by the

British governmental and military administration for Palestine, while the rest of the building continued to function as a hotel. The attack killed 41 Arabs, 28 Britons, and 17 Jews.

248 Greg Philo and Mike Berry, *More Bad News from Israel* (London: Pluto, 2011), 29.

In response to the bombing of the King David Hotel, Hecht wrote: "Every time you let go with your guns at the British betrayers of your homeland, the Jews of America make a little holiday in their hearts… Brave friends, we are working to help you. We are raising funds for you." (Lilienthal, *What Price Israel*, 33)

249 Lilienthal, *What Price Israel*, 79.

250 Lilienthal, *What Price Israel*, 79.

251 Howe, "Fighting the 'Soldiers of Occupation' From WWII to the Intifada."

252 Others were the Hebrew Committee for National Liberation, the Committee for a Jewish Army of Palestinian and Stateless Jews, the Hebrew Committee for National Liberation, and League for a Free Palestine. (Gurock, *American Zionism*, 386)

253 Rafael Medoff, "The Bergson Group vs. The Holocaust – and Jewish Leaders vs. Bergson," *The Jewish Press,* June 6, 2007,
http://www.jewishpress.com/pageroute.do/21747.

Among the groups they formed were American League for a Free Palestine, Hebrew Committee for National Liberation, and the Emergency Committee for the Rescue of European Jewry, often with a dual message: demanding the rescue of European Jews and the opening up of Palestine to Jewish immigration. Most Zionist and anti-Zionist organizations opposed the Bergson group, but it managed to enlist a number of prominent Americans, from Ben Hecht to Eleanor Roosevelt.

David S. Wyman, "The Bergson Group, America, and the Holocaust: A Previously Unpublished Interview with Hillel Kook/Peter Bergson," *American Jewish History* 89, No. 1 (2009), 3-34. Print. Online at http://muse.jhu.edu/login?auth=0&type=summary&url=/journals/american_jewish_history/v089/89.1wyman.html.

"The Irgun Abroad: Activities in Europe Before World War Two," The Irgun Site, accessed January 1, 2014, http://www.etzel.org.il/english/ac16.htm.

The United States Holocaust Memorial Museum states:

"Bergson's primary assignment in the United States was to mobilize support for the IZL and for the creation of Jewish military units, and, later to gather support for the creation of a Jewish state in Palestine. Bergson set out to accomplish these tasks by creating a series of interlocking organizations, including the Committee for a Jewish Army of Stateless and Palestinian Jews, the American League for a Free Palestine, the Emergency Committee to Save the Jewish People of Europe, and the Hebrew Committee for National Liberation."

"Peter Bergson," United States Holocaust Memorial Museum, accessed January 1, 2014, http://www.ushmm.org/wlc/en/article.php?ModuleId =10007041.

[254] Baumel, *The "Bergson Boys,"* 268-270.

[255] Medoff, *Militant Zionism*, 158.

[256] "Peter Bergson."

[257] Medoff, *Militant Zionism*, 192.

Ben Hecht also mentions this funding in his article praising Zionist violence against the British, "Letter to the Terrorists of Palestine," published on page 42 of the May 14, 1947 edition of the *New York Herald Tribune*: "Brave friends we are working to help you. We are raising money for you." (Philo and Berry, *More Bad News from Israel,* 29)

[258] Baumel, *The "Bergson Boys,"* xix.

[259] For some of their violence against Jews and others in Palestine, see Mark A Raider, "Irresponsible, Undisciplined Opposition: Ben Halpern on the Bergson Group and Jewish Terrorism in Pre-State Palestine," *American Jewish History* 92.3 (2004), 313-60.

[260] Baumel, *The "Bergson Boys,"* 114-115.

[261] Baumel, *The "Bergson Boys,"* 219-220.

Judah Magnes, a Reform rabbi, favored a binational state in which Jews and Palestinians would coexist in friendly relations.

[262] William D. Rubinstein, The Myth of Rescue: Why the Democracies Could Not Have Saved More Jews from the Nazis (London: Routledge, 1997), 97.

[263] Rubinstein, *Myth of Rescue*, 98.

264 Robert N. Rosen, *Saving the Jews: Franklin D. Roosevelt and the Holocaust* (New York: Thunder's Mouth, 2006), 32.

265 Baumel, *The "Bergson Boys,"* 261. See also Rubinstein, *Myth of Rescue*, 98.

266 Baumel, *The "Bergson Boys,"* 174.

267 Baumel, *The "Bergson Boys,"* 274.

268 Baumel, *The "Bergson Boys,"* 123.

269 Baumel, *The "Bergson Boys,"* 258-259.

270 Medoff, *Militant Zionism*, 186.

271 Baumel, *The "Bergson Boys,"* 225.

272 "Israel Independence Day: The Balfour Declaration," RavKookTorah.org, accessed January 1, 2014, http://www.ravkooktorah.org/YOM_ATZMAUT_66. htm.

273 "Time line for Rav Avraham Yitzchak HaKohen Kook," RavKookTorah.org, accessed January 1, 2014, http://www.ravkooktorah.org/timeline.htm.

"Israel Independence Day: The Balfour Declaration," RavKookTorah.org, accessed February 9, 2014,

http://ravkooktorah.org/YOM_ATZMAUT_66.htm.

Jay Levinson, "House of HaRav Avraham Yitzchak Kook," *Jewish Magazine*, March 2006,

http://www.jewishmag.com/100mag/kook/kook.htm.

Kabbala is also spelled: Cabbala, Cabala, Kabala.

Israel Shahak and Norton Mezvinsky, *Jewish Fundamentalism in Israel* (London: Pluto, 1999), ix, xiii, 55-69.

Professors Shahak and Mezvinsky emphasize that writings in English intentionally obscure many facts. "The role of Satan, whose earthly embodiment according to the Cabbala is every non-Jew, has been minimized or not mentioned by authors who have not written about the Cabbala in Hebrew." (Shahak and Mezvinsky, *Jewish Fundamentalism*, 58)

"According to the Lurianic Cabbala, the world was created solely for the sake of Jews; the existence of non-Jews was subsidiary."

Dr. Israel Shahak, was a holocaust survivor and, until his death in 2001, a highly regarded Israeli professor of biochemistry; Dr. Norton Mezvinsky was a professor of history (now retired) who in 2002 was named by the Connecticut State University Board of Trustees an official "Connecticut State University Professor...a signal honor, reserved for faculty members who fulfill the highest ideals of outstanding teaching, scholarly achievement and public service."

Another important book on this subject matter, by Israel Shahak, *Jewish History, Jewish Religion: the Weight of Three Thousand Years* (London: Pluto, 1997) can be read at

http://ifamericansknew.org/cur_sit/shahak.html.

274 Shahak and Mezvinsky, *Jewish Fundamentalism*, 55-69.

275 Shahak and Mezvinsky, *Jewish Fundamentalism*, ix.

Allan C. Brownfeld, review of *Jewish Fundamentalism in Israel*, by Israel Shahak and Norton Mezvinsky, *Washington Report on Middle East Affairs* March (2000): 105-06. Print. Online at http://www.ifamericansknew.org/history/rel-jfund.html.

[276] Baumel, *The "Bergson Boys,"* 256.

[277] Korff had emigrated to the U.S. in 1926 from the Ukraine. San Francisco's *Jewish Weekly* reports that he "was a link in an unbroken chain of rabbis in his family that dated back to the 11th century scholar Rashi. Another ancestor was the Baal Shem Tov, the 18th century founder of the Chassidic Movement."-

Avi V. Stieglitz, "Baruch Korff, 'Nixon's Rabbi' and Activist, Dies of Cancer at 81." *JWeekly,* August 4, 1995. Print. Online at http://www.jweekly.com/article/full/1382/baruch-korff-nixon-s-rabbi-and-activist-dies-of-cancer-at-81/.

[278] Medoff, *Militant Zionism,* 164.

"The Bergson Group: A History in Photographs," David S. Wyman Institute for Holocaust Studies, accessed December 19, 2013, http://wymaninstitute.org/special/bergsonexhibit/leadership5.php.

[279] Medoff, *Militant Zionism,* 165.

[280] Medoff, *Militant Zionism,* 166.

[281] Medoff, *Militant Zionism,* 166.

[282] Neil Tweedie and Peter Day, "Jewish Groups Plotted to Kill Bevin," *Telegraph,* May 22, 2003. Print. Online at http://www.telegraph.co.uk/news/1430766/Jewish-groups-plotted-to-kill-Bevin.html.

"MI5 Feared Zionist Air Raid Plan for London," *The Journal* (Northumberland), May 22, 2003, http://www.thefreelibrary.com/MI5+feared+Zionist+air+raid+plan+for+London.-a0102133325.

"Possible Jewish Terrorist Attempts to Assassinate Ernest Bevin, Foreign Secretary," UK Government Official Archives, October 31, 1945 - August 17, 1946, http://discovery.nationalarchives.gov.uk/SearchUI/details/C11602817?uri=C11602817-details.

Download at http://discovery.nationalarchives.gov.uk/SearchUI/image/Index/C11602817.

[283] "French Arresting Irgun, Sternist Aides After Exposure of Alleged Plot to Bomb London," *Jewish Telegraphic Agency*, September 8, 1947, http://www.jta.org/1947/09/08/archive/french-arresting-irgun-sternist-aides-after-exposure-of-alleged-plot-to-bomb-london.

[284] Information on this section comes from news reports from the time, a UN report which seems to have disappeared from the UN archives, a first-person account written by Gilbert himself distributed by the New York Herald Tribune, and Gilbert's unpublished memoir. He also discussed it with the author by phone and in person in 2012.

"Timeline of Zionist Terror," UN Report Prepared in 1948 for Ralph Bunche, New UN Commissioner to Palestine (New York: October 1, 1948), accessed January 1, 2014, http://www.al-nakba-history.com/origins1948/unterrorismchronology.html.

[285] Unpublished memoir by Reginald Gilbert, 118-127.

"Flyer Credited With Expose of Bombing Plans," *Daily Mail* (Hagerstown, MD) September 9, 1947, 1. Print. Online at http://newspaperarchive.com/hagerstown-daily-mail/1947-09-09/.

The Stern Gang, also called Stern Group or Lehi, formally Loḥamei Ḥerut Yisra'el (Hebrew: "Fighters for the Freedom of Israel"), was a Zionist terrorist organization founded in 1940 by Avraham Stern after a split in the Irgun. The *Encyclopaedia Britannica* reports: "Extremely anti-British, the group repeatedly attacked British personnel in Palestine and even invited aid from the Axis powers."

"Stern Gang," *Encyclopaedia Britannica*, accessed January 1, 2014, http://www.britannica.com/EBchecked/topic/565756/Stern-Gang.

[286] UP, "French Judge Weighs Bomb Plot," *Lima News* (Lima, OH), September 8, 1947, 1. Print. Online at http://newspaperarchive.com/lima-news/1947-09-08/.

AP, "Hold Rabbi for Questioning in 'Leaflet Bombing' Plot," *Schenectady Gazette*, September 9, 1940, 1. Print. Online at http://news.google.com/newspapers?nid=1917&dat=19470909&id=9EohAAAAIBAJ&sjid=gYEFAAAAIBAJ&pg=3436,984641.

AP, "Yank Flyer Reveals Stern Gang Hired Him to Drop Bombs on British Foreign Office," *St. Petersburg Times,* September 10, 1947, 1. Print. Online at http://news.google.com/newspapers?nid=888&dat=1 9470910&id=8VtIAAAAIBAJ&sjid=3E4DAAAAIBA J&pg=2421,4272387.

A.A.P. and Argus correspondent, "US pilot told police of bomb plot, was asked to raid London," *The Argus* (Melbourne), September 9, 1947, 1. Print. Online at http://trove.nla.gov.au/ndp/del/article/22506150.

287 A.A.P. "Jewish Terror plot Unearthed," *Sydney Morning Herald*, September 8, 1947, 1. Print. Online at http://trove.nla.gov.au/ndp/del/article/18042464.

David Perlman, "U.S. War Ace Foiled Plot to Bomb London," *New York Herald Tribune*, 1947.

288 Reginald Gilbert, "St. Louis Pilot Tells How and Why He Foiled Plot to Bomb London," *New York Herald Tribune*, September 9, 1947.

Gilbert, unpublished memoir. Personal interview with author.

289 "1947:Stern Gang Foiled : In our Pages:100, 75 And 50 Years Ago," *New York Times*, September 9, 1997, http://www.nytimes.com/1997/09/09/opinion/09iht-edold.t_20.html

290 UP, "Jews Say Bomb Plot Was British Frameup," *Lebanon Daily News* (Lebanon, PA), September 11, 1947, 17. Print. Online at http://newspaperarchive.com/lebanon-daily-news/1947-09-10/page-17.

291 "Early Release of Rabbi Korff Expected in Paris; U.S. Embassy Makes No Official Move," *Jewish Telegraphic Agency*, September 18, 1947,

http://archive.jta.org/article/1947/09/18/3011591/ea
rly-release-of-rabbi-korff-expected-in-paris-us-embassy-
makes-no-official-move.

292 "Question Authenticity Police Version of Plot,"
Canadian Jewish Chronicle, September 26, 1947, 4. Print.
Online at
http://news.google.com/newspapers?nid=883&dat=1
9470926&id=jQFPAAAAIBAJ&sjid=jEwDAAAAIB
AJ&pg=904,4915328.

293 "Zionists Plotted IRA-style Terrorism," *Times*
(London), May 22, 2003,
http://www.thetimes.co.uk/tto/news/uk/article19087
76.ece.

294 A.A.P. "Release of Rabbi Sought," *Advertiser* (Adelaide,
SA), September 10, 1947, 1. Print. Online at
http://trove.nla.gov.au/ndp/del/article/35998232.

Medoff, *Militant Zionism,* 170. Medoff's account only
mentions the part of the plan to do with dropping
pamphlets. He omits any mention of Gilbert and of the
attempted assassination aspect of the plot.

295 "Rabbi Jacob Israel Korff," Find a Grave, accessed
January 1, 2014, http://www.findagrave.com/cgi-
bin/fg.cgi?page=gr&GRid=110684672.

"Grand Rabbi Jacob Israel Korff: The Zviller
Rebbe," Paul Gass Family website, accessed January 1,
2014,
http://www.paulgassfamily.com/section3/iii1/iii1_001
.htm.

296 Stevens, *American Zionism,* 192.

297 Eric Pace, "Baruch Korff, 81, Rabbi and Defender of Nixon," *New York Times*, July 27, 1995, http://www.nytimes.com/1995/07/27/obituaries/baruch-korff-81-rabbi-and-defender-of-nixon.html.

298 Stieglitz, "Baruch Korff, 'Nixon's Rabbi' and Activist, Dies of Cancer at 81."

"...Korff had many supporters in high places in Israel, including Yitzhak Rabin and the formidable Golda Meir. As the Israeli Prime Minister during the Yom Kippur war of 1973 she was immensely grateful to Nixon, with whom she struck up an unlikely though fateful friendship, for the giant American airlift which helped to turn defeat into victory."

Joseph Finkelstone, "Obituaries: Rabbi Baruch Korff," *Independent* (UK), August 3, 1995, http://www.independent.co.uk/news/people/obituaries-rabbi-baruch-korff-1594514.html.

299 Bob Woodward and Carl Bernstein, *The Final Days* (New York: Simon and Schuster, 1976), 101.

300 AP, "Rabbi Korff Announces Retirement from Nixon Fund," *Spartanburg Herald-Journal*, May 29, 1975, 12. Print. Online at http://news.google.com/newspapers?nid=1876&dat=19750529&id=f5QeAAAAIBAJ&sjid=HcwEAAAAIBAJ&pg=7086,5202171.

301 Stieglitz, "Baruch Korff, 'Nixon's Rabbi' and Activist, Dies of Cancer at 81."

302 Finkelstone, "Obituaries: Rabbi Baruch Korff."

Others also note Korff's access to powerful leaders:

Henry Morgenthau, *Mostly Morgenthaus: A Family History* (New York: Ticknor & Fields, 1991). Excerpt online at http://www.paulgassfamily.com/section3/iii3/iii3_003.htm#_ftnref5.

Morgenthau calls Korff a "wily expediter," writing: "At a very early age Rabbi Korff had gained the ear and confidence of many prominent American politicians, winning special access to Congressman John McCormack of Massachusetts (then House majority leader, later Speaker) and Senator James M. Mead of New York (the best man at Korff's wedding)."

Prominent columnist Mary McGrory described an event in 1978 attended by generals and high-ranking US Senators.

Mary McGrory, "Return Engagement for Rabbi Korff," *St. Petersburg Times*, March 1, 1978, 12. Print. Online at http://news.google.com/newspapers?nid=888&dat=19780301&id=oTYpAAAAIBAJ&sjid=s1kDAAAAIBAJ&pg=2729,94958.

[303] Leonard Slater, *The Pledge* (New York: Simon and Schuster, 1970), 21-23.

Smith, Declassified Deceptions, Chapter 4.

[304] Slater, *Pledge*, 23.

[305] Slater, *Pledge*, 24.

[306] Smith, Declassified Deceptions, 63.

An active supporter of the United Jewish Appeal in the 1940s describes raising money for weapons: "Any contributions that were made had to be made in cash...

It was a sort of a hush-hush operation because it was not entirely legal."

"Ties that Bind: Washington Area Jews and the Birth of the State of Israel," Jewish Historical Society of Greater Washington, accessed January 1, 2014, http://www.jhsgw.org/israel60/slideshow/secret-meetings.php.

"Local members of the clandestine Sonneborn Institute held secret meetings to raise money for a Jewish state and its underground army, the Haganah."

"Securing the Dream," Jewish Historical Society of Greater Washington, accessed January 1, 2014, http://www.jhsgw.org/exhibitions/online/jewishwashi ngton/exhibition/securing-the-dream.

The local Zionist youth group, Habonim, helped load weapons onto ships.

"Ties that Bind: Washington Area Jews and the Birth of the State of Israel," Jewish Historical Society of Greater Washington, accessed January 1, 2014, http://www.jhsgw.org/israel60/slideshow/habonim-march.php.

Habonim camps are still active today, with seven summer camps across Canada and the US, an Israel summer program, and a year-long program based in Israel. See https://www.habonimdror.org.

[307] Smith, *Declassified Deceptions*, 37.

R.H. Hillenkoetter, "Memorandum for the Secretary of Defense: Subject: Clandestine Air Transport Operations," *Central Intelligence Agency*, May 28, 1948. Print. Online at

http://www.foia.cia.gov/sites/default/files/document
_conversions/89801/DOC_0000655104.pdf.

308 Smith, Declassified Deceptions, 37.

Grant Smith also covers these groups in detail in his book, *Spy Trade: How Israel's Lobby Undermines America's Economy* (Washington D.C.: IRMEP, 2008). Smith writes: "The organizations and individuals in the Sonneborn Institute's network all engaged in legitimate charitable activities as well as theft and smuggling. This cover and connection to elites involved across U.S. politics, business, and government made it a difficult target for law enforcement." (Smith, *Spy Trade*, 25)

Smith reports that while a few operatives were imprisoned or fined for their activities, "...none of the truly 'big fish' of the Sonneborn arms smuggling network were ever indicted." Henry Montor, the person who organized the first meeting, headed up the United Jewish Appeal and later founded the Israel Bond organization. (Smith, *Spy Trade*, 24)

William Levitt of the famous "Levittown" housing development, gave the Haganah a million dollars interest-free loan to buy fighter aircraft from Czechoslovakia was never prosecuted for violating the Neutrality Act. (Smith, *Spy Trade*, 24)

Smith reports that the only person to serve an appropriate prison sentence was posthumously pardoned by President George W. Bush after intense lobbying by Steven Spielberg and others. (Smith, *Spy Trade*, 25)

[309] *New York Times*, August 10, 1961. Conversion was done using Areppin calculator:
http://stats.areppim.com/calc/calc_usdlrxdeflxcpi.php

[310] Grodzinsky, *Shadow of the Holocaust*, 9.

[311] Grodzinsky, *Shadow of the Holocaust*, 9.

[312] The first survey among Jewish survivors found that 65 percent indicated that they wished to return home, 20 percent wished to go to the US, and 15 percent desired to go to Palestine. (Grodzinsky, *Shadow of the Holocaust*, 41) The Mossad commander was Ze'ev Schind, alias "Danny." (Grodzinsky, *Shadow of the Holocaust*, 48)

[313] Lilienthal, *What Price Israel*, 148-150.

[314] "Jewish Brigade Group," United States Holocaust Memorial Museum, accessed January 1, 2014, http://www.ushmm.org/wlc/en/article.php?ModuleId=10005275.

[315] Grodzinsky, *Shadow of the Holocaust*, 49.

[316] Grodzinsky, *Shadow of the Holocaust*, 50.

[317] Grodzinsky, *Shadow of the Holocaust*, 50. Citation: "An interview with Ms. Fanny Tirosh (Yossie Peled's and Sarah Gutman's sister), an addendum to ha-Mifgash (The Encounter), Tel-Aviv: Daniela Dinnur, pp. 115-116, 1993. An appendix contains attestations by Peled and his sisters, and of the daughter of the adopting Belgian who had saved them."

[318] Grodzinsky, *Shadow of the Holocaust*, 50-51.

[319] Grodzinsky, *Shadow of the Holocaust*, 52.

[320] Baruch Kimmerling, "Israel's Culture of Martyrdom." *The Nation,* January 10, 2005. Online at

http://www.thenation.com/article/israels-culture-martyrdom?page=full.

Zertal, Idith. *Israel's Holocaust and the Politics of Nationhood.* Cambridge, UK: Cambridge University Press, 2005, 51

321 Baruch Kimmerling, "Israel's Culture of Martyrdom." *The Nation,* January 10, 2005. Online at http://www.thenation.com/article/israels-culture-martyrdom?page=full.

This was not the only such case that has been somewhat misrepresented in Zionist propaganda. Two hundreds Jewish refugees aboard another such ship, the *Patria*, died when Jewish forces placed a bomb under the hull to disable the ship. – Charles Smith, 115.

322 Grodzinsky, 226.

323 Grodzinsky, *Shadow of the Holocaust*, 199, 203.

324 Grodzinsky, *Shadow of the Holocaust*, 210.

325 Grodzinsky *Shadow of the Holocaust*, 212-214.

326 Segev, *Seventh Million*, 34.

327 Grose, *Mind of America*, 207-210.

Sir Frederick Morgan described the situation in detail in a chapter of his autobiography, "A 'Displaced Person' in Post-War Germany," in *Peace and War: A Soldier's Life* (London: Hodder and Stoughton, 1961), 234-38, 243-62. Excerpted in Khalidi, *Haven To Conquest*, 527-548.

Morgan reported that "the admirably organized Zionist command was employing any and every means of forcing immigration into the country irrespective of the hardship and sufferings of the immigrants, few of whom seemed to have any spontaneous enthusiasm for the Zionist cause." (Morgan, "Displaced Person," 533) Morgan described the "consummate skill" with which the Zionist organizations pushed their propaganda, and noted that Eddie Cantor had announced in a full page ad in the New York Times that Morgan was "no less than a reincarnation of the late A. Hitler." (Morgan, "Displaced Person," 532)

328 Grose, *Mind of America*, 177.

329 Grose, *Mind of America*, 178-182.

330 For details, see The Ethnic Cleansing of Palestine by Ilan Pappe and Under the Cover of War: The Zionist Expulsion of the Palestinians by Rosemarie M. Esber.

331 Neff, *Pillars*, 68.

332 Neff, *Pillars*, 69.

Transjordan's entire government budget at the time was only $5 million.

333 Neff, *Pillars*, 69.

334 Neff, *Pillars*, 72. Neff, *Pillars*, 72. Currency conversion: http://www.dollartimes.com/calculators/inflation.htm.

335 Anders Strindberg, "Forgotten Christians," *American Conservative*, May 24, 2004, http://www.amconmag.com/article/2004/may/24/00 013/.

336 Interestingly, Truman had hoped for what is today called the "one state solution." According to Grose, on the day that Israel declared itself a state and Truman provided it immediate recognition, Truman wrote to a friend: "The correct solution" would be a single state in which Jews and Arabs would share power. He

continued, "and, I think, eventually we are going to get it worked out just that way."

Peter Grose, "Truman and Israel," *Moment* 8, no. 6 (June 1983): 19. Online at http://search.opinionarchives.com/Summary/Moment/V8I6P13-1.htm.

337 Neff, *Pillars*, 75.

338 Neff, *Pillars*, 76-77. Citation: George McGhee, *Envoy to the Middle World: Adventures in Diplomacy* (New York: Harper & Row, 1983), 37.

339 Richard D. McKinzie, "Oral History Interview with Edwin M. Wright," The interview was conducted in Wooster, Ohio on July 26, 1974. On April 3, 1977, Wright added a letter and footnotes to the interview. Online at http://www.trumanlibrary.org/oralhist/wright.htm.

340 Stevens, *American Zionism*, 207.

341 Christison, *Perceptions*, 38.

342 Christison, *Perceptions*, 40.

343 Neff, *Pillars*, 67.

344 Neff, *Pillars*, 72-73.

A notable exception were the reports by Anne O'Hare McCormick, a Pulitzer Prize winning foreign news correspondent for the *New York Times*, who reported that "[Israel] is born at the expense of another people now fated to join the ragged ranks of the displaced" and, in another reported, noted that "no one [in Israel] has expressed any sense of responsibility or sympathy for these wretched victims."

345 Lilienthal, *What Price Israel*, 94.

346 Lilienthal, *What Price Israel*, 103.

347 Lilienthal, *What Price Israel*, 94.

348 Christison, *Perceptions*, 80-81.

349 Lilienthal, *What Price Israel*, 96-97.

350 Lilienthal, *What Price Israel*, 97-98.

351 Millar Burrows, *Palestine Is Our Business* (Philadelphia: Westminster, 1949), 11.

352 Burrows, *Palestine Is Our Business*, 11-12.

353 Burrows, *Palestine Is Our Business*, 63.

354 Burrows, *Palestine Is Our Business*, 75.

355 Burrows, *Palestine Is Our Business*, 131.

356 Burrows, Palestine Is Our Business, 91.

357 Burrows, *Palestine Is Our Business*, 154.

358 Burrows, *Palestine Is Our Business*, 155.

359 Lilienthal, *What Price Israel*, 97-98.

360 Lilienthal, *What Price Israel*, 97.

361 Berger, *Memoirs*, 35-38.

Dean Gildersleeve, a Protestant Christian, had been the only woman member of the U.S. UN delegation in San Francisco. For more information on her see:

"Who was Virginia Gildersleeve?" *Virginia Gildersleeve International Fund*, accessed December 20, 2013, http://www.vgif.org/a_vg.shtml.

Rosalind Rosenberg, "Virginia Gildersleeve: Opening the Gates," *Living Legacies* (Columbia University), accessed January 1, 2014, http://www.columbia.edu/cu/alumni/Magazine/Summer2001/Gildersleeve.html.

362 Virginia Crocheron Gildersleeve, *Many a Good Crusade: Memoirs of* (New York: Macmillan, 1955), 187.

363 Merkley, Christian Attitudes, 7.

364 Gildersleeve, *Many a Good Crusade,* 412.

365 "Dorothy Thompson," *Encyclopaedia Britannica Online*, accessed January 1, 2014, http://www.britannica.com/EBchecked/topic/592960 /Dorothy-Thompson.

366 The information from this section comes largely from *American Cassandra: The Life of Dorothy Thompson* by Peter Kurth, "Remembering Dorothy Thompson" by Peter Kurth (online at http://www.ifamericansknew.org/media/dthompson.h tml), *Dorothy Thompson: A Legend in her Time* by Marion K. Sanders, *Personal History* by Vincent Sheean, *Dorothy & Red* (Dorothy Thompson & Sinclair Lewis) by Vincent Sheean, and Elmer Berger's *Memoirs*, 62-70. See also http://thesilencing.org/.

367 *Sands of Sorrow*, produced by Council for the Relief of Palestine Arab Refugees, narrated by Dorothy Thompson, 1950, http://www.youtube.com/watch?v=lQ6lIsl-pHU. Also available at http://www.archive.org/details/sands_of_sorrow.

368 Kurth, American Cassandra, 384.

369 Kurth, American Cassandra, 384.

370 "The Press: Free Speech for the Boss," *Time*, November 17, 1958, accessed January 1, 2014, http://www.time.com/time/magazine/article/0,9171,8 10661,00.html.

371 Kurth, American Cassandra, 383.

[372] A nonprofit organization is currently working on a film on Thompson, which they hope to release in 2014 or 15. See http://thesilencing.org/.

[373] George Orwell, *Nineteen Eighty-four* (New York: Harcourt, Brace, 1949), 88.

Interestingly, a biographer states: "In his last years, unlike several of his comrades around *Tribune*, Orwell had little sympathy with Zionism and opposed the creation of the state of Israel, as attested by his friend and *Tribune* colleague Tosco Fyvel in his book *George Orwell: A Personal Memoir*."

"George Orwell Biography," Orwell Web, accessed January 1, 2014,
http://www.netcharles.com/orwell/articles/george-orwell-biography.htm.

Another discussion is here:
http://evenements.univ-lille3.fr/colloque-george-orwell/abstracts/samedi-09h30.pdf.

WORKS CITED

"1947: Stern Gang Foiled: In Our Pages: 100, 75 And 50 Years Ago." *New York Times*, September 9, 1997. http://www.nytimes.com/1997/09/09/opinion/09iht-edold.t_20.html.

"Abraham Feinberg's FBI File." The Israel Lobby Archive. Accessed January 1, 2014. http://www.irmep.org/ila/feinberg/.

Abu-Sitta, Salman H. *Atlas of Palestine, 1917-1966*. London: Palestine Land Society, 2010.

Alexander, Michael. *Jazz Age Jews*. Princeton, NJ: Princeton UP, 2001.

"American Zionist Movement (AZM)." Jewish Virtual Library. 2008. Accessed January 1, 2014. http://www.jewishvirtuallibrary.org/jsource/judaica/ejud_0002_0002_0_00978.html.

Anson, Daphne. "The Mosque-Founder's Nephew Who Drafted the Balfour Declaration – Leopold Amery, the 'Secret Jew'" *Daphne Anson Blog* (web log), November 1, 2010. http://daphneanson.blogspot.com/2010/10/mosque-founders-nephew-who-drafted.html.

Arendt, Hannah, and Albert Einstein Et Al. "New Palestine Party." *New York Times*, December 4, 1948,

Letters Sec. Online at
http://www.globalwebpost.com/farooqm/study_res
/einstein/nyt_orig.html.

"The Assassination of Count Bernadotte." Jewish Virtual
Library. Accessed January 1, 2014.
http://www.jewishvirtuallibrary.org/jsource/History
/folke.html.

"Balfour Declaration Author Was a Secret Jew, Says
Prof." *Jweekly* (San Francisco), January 15, 1999.
http://www.jweekly.com/article/full/9929/balfour-
declaration-author-was-a-secret-jew-says-prof.

Ball, George W., and Douglas B. Ball. *The Passionate
Attachment: America's Involvement with Israel, 1947 to the
Present.* New York: W.W. Norton, 1992.

Barrett, Mary. "In Memoriam: A Respectful Dissenter:
CIA's Wilbur Crane Eveland." *Washington Report on
Middle East Affairs,* March 1990, 28.
http://www.wrmea.org/wrmea-archives/125-
washington-report-archives-1988-1993/march-
1990/1077-in-memoriam-wilbur-crane-eveland.html.

Baumel-Schwartz, Judith Tydor. *The "Bergson Boys" and the
Origins of Contemporary Zionist Militancy.* Syracuse, NY:
Syracuse University Press, 2005.

Beisner, Robert L. *Dean Acheson: A Life in the Cold War.*
Oxford: Oxford University Press, 2006.

Beit-Hallahmi, Benjamin. *Original Sins: Reflections on the
History of Zionism and Israel.* New York: Olive Branch
Press, 1993.

Berg, A. Scott. *Wilson.* New York: G.P. Putnam's Sons,
2013.

Berger, Elmer. *Memoirs of an Anti-Zionist Jew.* Beirut:
Institute for Palestine Studies, 1978.

"The Bergson Group: A History in Photographs." David S. Wyman Institute for Holocaust Studies. Accessed December 20, 2013. http://wymaninstitute.org/special/bergsonexhibit/leadership5.php.

British Mandatory Commission. *A Survey of Palestine: Prepared in December 1945 and January 1946 for the Information of the Anglo-American Committee of Inquiry.* Washington, D.C.: Institute for Palestine Studies, 1991.

Brownfeld, Allan C. Review of *Jewish Fundamentalism in Israel,* by Israel Shahak and Norton Mezvinsky. *Washington Report on Middle East Affairs* March (2000): 105-06.

Brym, Robert. Review of *Zionism and Territory: The Socio-Territorial Dimensions of Zionist Politics,* by Baruch Kimmerling. *The Canadian Journal of Sociology* 11, no. 1 (1986): 79-82.

Burrows, Millar. *Palestine Is Our Business.* Philadelphia: Westminster Press, 1949.

Campbell, John C. Review of *Israel in the Mind of America,* by Peter Grose. *Foreign Affairs,* Spring 1984. http://www.foreignaffairs.com/articles/38470/john-c-campbell/israel-in-the-mind-of-america.

Canfield, Joseph M. *The Incredible Scofield and His Book.* Vallecito, CA: Ross House Books, 2004.

Cantor, Norman F. *The Jewish Experience.* New York: HarperCollins, 1996.

Cattan, Henry. *The Palestine Question.* London: Croom Helm, 1988.

Central Intelligence Agency. *The Consequences of the Partition of Palestine.* Report. Vol. 55. ORE. 1947.

Childers, Erskine. "The Other Exodus." *The Spectator*, May 12, 1961, 672-75. http://www.users.cloud9.net/~recross/israel-watch/ErskinChilders.html.

Chomsky, Noam. *The Fateful Triangle: The United States, Israel, and the Palestinians*. Boston, MA: South End Press, 1983.

Christison, Kathleen. *Perceptions of Palestine: Their Influence on U.S. Middle East Policy*. 1st ed. Berkeley, CA: University of California Press, 2000.

Coffin, William Sloane. *The Collected Sermons of William Sloane Coffin: The Riverside Years*. Vol. 1. Louisville, KY: Westminster John Knox Press, 2008.

Cohen, Naomi W. *The Americanization of Zionism, 1897-1948*. Hanover: Brandeis University Press, 2003.

Collins, Larry, and Dominique Lapierre. *O Jerusalem*. New York: Simon and Schuster, 1972.

Cornelius, John. "The Balfour Declaration and the Zimmermann Note." *Washington Report on Middle East Affairs*, August/September 1997, 18-20. http://www.wrmea.org/wrmea-archives/188-washington-report-archives-1994-1999/august-september-1997/2646-the-balfour-declaration-and-the-zimmermann-note-.html.

Cornelius, John. "The Hidden History of the Balfour Declaration." *Washington Report on Middle East Affairs*, November 2005, 44-50. http://www.wrmea.com/component/content/article/278-2005-november/8356-special-report-the-hidden-history-of-the-balfour-declaration.html.

Curtiss, Richard H., and Janet McMahon. *Seeing the Light: Personal Encounters with the Middle East and Islam*.

Washington, D.C.: American Educational Trust, 1997.

Curtiss, Richard H. "Truman Adviser Recalls May 14, 1948 US Decision to Recognize Israel." *Washington Report on Middle East Affairs*, May/June 1991, 17. http://www.wrmea.org/wrmea-archives/131-washington-report-archives-1988-1993/may-june-1991/1634-truman-adviser-recalls-may-141948-us-decision-to-recognize-israel.html.

Davidson, Lawrence. *America's Palestine: Popular and Official Perceptions from Balfour to Israeli Statehood.* Gainesville, FL: University Press of Florida, 2001.

Davidson, Lawrence. "Truman the Politician and the Establishment of Israel." *Journal of Palestine Studies* 39, no. 4 (2010): 28-42. http://www.palestine-studies.org/journals.aspx?id=10710&jid=1&href=full text.

Davis, John Herbert. *The Evasive Peace: A Study of the Zionist-Arab Problem.* 1st American Ed. New York: New World, 1970.

De Haas, Jacob. *Louis D. Brandeis: A Biographical Sketch: With Special Reference to His Contributions to Jewish and Zionist History: With Full Text of His Addresses Delivered from 1912 to 1924.* New York: Bloch, 1929. doi:ark:/13960/t6zw19f6x.

"Early Release of Rabbi Korff Expected in Paris; U.S. Embassy Makes No Official Move." *Jewish Telegraphic Agency* (New York), September 18, 1947. http://archive.jta.org/article/1947/09/18/3011591/early-release-of-rabbi-korff-expected-in-paris-us-embassy-makes-no-official-move.

Encyclopaedia Britannica Online. Accessed January 1, 2014. http://www.britannica.com/EBchecked/topic/565756/Stern-Gang.

Encyclopaedia Britannica Online. Accessed January 1, 2014. http://www.britannica.com/EBchecked/topic/5929 60/Dorothy-Thompson.

Esber, Rosemarie M. *Under the Cover of War: The Zionist Expulsion of the Palestinians.* Alexandria, VA: Arabicus Books & Media, 2008.

Eveland, Wilbur. *Ropes of Sand: America's Failure in the Middle East.* London: W.W. Norton, 1980.

Fattah, Hala. "Sultan Abdul-Hamid and the Zionist Colonization of Palestine." March 11, 1999. http://www.lahana.org/blog/Zionist%20Colonizatio n%20of%20Palestine.htm.

Feinberg, Abraham. "Abraham Feinberg Oral History Interview." Interview by Richard D. McKinzie. Harry S. Truman Library and Museum. August 23, 1973. http://www.trumanlibrary.org/oralhist/feinberg.htm.

Finkelstein, Norman G. *Beyond Chutzpah: On the Misuse of Anti-Semitism and the Abuse of History.* Berkeley: University of California Press, 2005.

Finkelstone, Joseph. "Obituaries: Rabbi Baruch Korff." *Independent* (London), August 3, 1995. http://www.independent.co.uk/news/people/obitua ries-rabbi-baruch-korff-1594514.html.

"Flyer Credited With Expose of Bombing Plans." *Daily Mail* (Hagerstown, MD), September 9, 1947. http://newspaperarchive.com/hagerstown-daily-mail/1947-09-09/.

"French Arresting Irgun, Sternist Aides After Exposure of Alleged Plot to Bomb London." *Jewish Telegraphic Agency* (New York), September 8, 1947. http://www.jta.org/1947/09/08/archive/french-arresting-irgun-sternist-aides-after-exposure-of-alleged-plot-to-bomb-london.

"French Judge Weighs Bomb Plot." *Lima News* (Lima, OH), September 8, 1947. http://newspaperarchive.com/lima-news/1947-09-08?tag=korff,york,denied&rtserp=tags/korff,york,denied?py=1947.

"George Orwell Biography." Orwell Web. Accessed January 1, 2014. http://www.netcharles.com/orwell/articles/george-orwell-biography.htm.

Gildersleeve, Virginia Crocheron. *Many a Good Crusade: Memoirs of.* New York: Macmillan, 1955.

Ginsberg, Benjamin. *The Fatal Embrace: Jews and the State.* Chicago: University of Chicago, 1993.

Glass, Charles. "The Mandate Years: Colonialism and the Creation of Israel." *The Guardian*, May 31, 2001. http://www.theguardian.com/books/2001/may/31/londonreviewofbooks/print.

Goldberg, Jonathan J. *Jewish Power: Inside the American Jewish Establishment.* Reading, MA: Addison-Wesley, 1996.

Grady, Henry. Chapter 9 of Unpublished Manuscript "Adventures in Diplomacy" MS, Harry S. Truman Library, Independence, MO. Accessed January 1, 2014. http://www.trumanlibrary.org/whistlestop/study_collections/israel/large/documents/index.php?documentdate=0000-00-00&documentid=4-7&studycollectionid=ROI&pagenumber=1.

Grady, Henry Francis, and John T. McNay. *The Memoirs of Ambassador Henry F. Grady: From the Great War to the Cold War.* Columbia, MO: University of Missouri Press, 2009.

"Grand Rabbi Jacob Israel Korff: The Zviller Rebbe." Paul Gass Family Website. Accessed January 1, 2014.

http://www.paulgassfamily.com/section3/iii1/iii1_0
01.htm.

Green, Stephen. *Taking Sides, America's Secret Relations with a Militant Israel.* Brattleboro: Amana Books, 1988.

Grodzinsky, Yosef, and Chris Spannos. "In the Shadow of the Holocaust." *Znet,* June 7, 2005. http://www.zcommunications.org/in-the-shadow-of-the-holocaust-by-yosef-grodzinsky.html.

Grodzinsky, Yosef. *In the Shadow of the Holocaust: The Struggle between Jews and Zionists in the Aftermath of World War II.* Monroe, ME: Common Courage Press, 2004.

Grose, Peter. *Israel in the Mind of America.* New York: Knopf, 1984.

Grose, Peter. "Louis Brandeis, Arthur Balfour and a Declaration That Made History." *Moment* 8, no. 10 (November 1983): 17-39. http://search.opinionarchives.com/Summary/Moment/V8I10P27-1.htm.

Grose, Peter. "Peter Grose Papers." MS MC227, Princeton University Library, Princeton, New Jersey. http://findingaids.princeton.edu/collections/MC227.

Grose, Peter. "Truman and Israel." *Moment,* June 1983. http://search.opinionarchives.com/Summary/Moment/V8I6P13-1.htm.

Gurock, Jeffrey S. *American Zionism: Missions and Politics.* London: Routledge, 1998. Google Books.

Hart, Alan. Zionism: The Real Enemy of the Jews. Atlanta, GA: Clarity Press, 2009.

Hadawi, Sami. *Bitter Harvest: Palestine Between 1914-1979.* New York: Caravan Books, 1979.

Herzl, Theodor. *The Jewish State.* New York: Dover Publications, 1988.

An unabridged, unaltered republication of the work originally published in 1946 by the American Zionist Emergency Council, New York, and edited by Jacob W. Alkow. The volume includes a translation of Herzl's 1896 "Der Judenstaat," an introduction by Louis Lipsky, and a biography of Herzl based on the work of Alex Bein.

Hillenkoetter, R. H. *Memorandum for the Secretary of Defense: Subject: Clandestine Air Transport Operations.* Report no. EO 12985 3.4 (b)(1). Washington, D.C.: Central Intelligence Agency, 1948. http://www.foia.cia.gov/sites/default/files/documen t_conversions/89801/DOC_0000655104.pdf.

"Hold Rabbi for Questioning in 'Leaflet Bombing' Plot." *Schenectady Gazette*, September 9, 1940. http://news.google.com/newspapers?nid=1917&dat =19470909&id=9EohAAAAIBAJ&sjid=gYEFAAA AIBAJ&pg=3436,984641.

Hoover, Herbert. "Message to the American Palestine Committee, January 17, 1932." The American Presidency Project. http://www.presidency.ucsb.edu/ws/?pid=23121.

Howard, Harry N. "Oral History Interview with Harry N. Howard." Interview by Richard D. McKinzie. Harry S. Truman Library and Museum. June 5, 1973. http://www.trumanlibrary.org/oralhist/howardhn.ht m.

Howe, Russell Warren, and Sarah Hays Trott. *The Power Peddlers: How Lobbyists Mold America's Foreign Policy.* Garden City, NY: Doubleday, 1977.

"The Irgun Abroad: Activities in Europe Before World War Two." The Irgun Site. Accessed January 1, 2014. http://www.etzel.org.il/english/ac16.htm.

"Israel Independence Day: The Balfour Declaration."
RavKookTorah.org. Accessed January 1, 2014.
http://www.ravkooktorah.org/YOM_ATZMAUT_6
6.htm.

"The Israel Lobby Archive." *Institute for Research: Middle
Eastern Policy.* http://irmep.org/ILA/default.asp.

Jeffries, J.M. N. *Palestine: The Reality.* London: Longmans,
Green and Co., 1939.

"Jewish Brigade Group." United States Holocaust
Memorial Museum. June 10, 2013.
http://www.ushmm.org/wlc/en/article.php?Module
Id=10005275.

"Jewish Terror Plot Unearthed." *Sydney Morning Herald,*
September 8, 1947.
http://trove.nla.gov.au/ndp/del/article/18042464.

"Jews Say Bomb Plot Was British Frameup." *Lebanon Daily
News* (Lebanon, PA), September 11, 1947.
http://newspaperarchive.com/lebanon-daily-
news/1947-09-10/page-17.

John, Robert and Sami Hadawi. *The Palestine Diary 1914-
1945 Britain's Involvement,* Vol. 1. Reprint of Third Ed.
Charleston: BookSurge, 2006.

Kauffman, Bill. *Ain't My America: The Long, Noble History of
Antiwar Conservatism and Middle American Anti-
imperialism.* New York: Metropolitan, 2008.

Khalidi, Walid. *All That Remains: The Palestinian Villages
Occupied and Depopulated by Israel in 1948.* Washington,
D.C.: Institute for Palestine Studies, 1992.

Khalidi, Walid. *From Haven to Conquest: Readings in Zionism
and the Palestine Problem until 1948.* Vol. 2. Washington,
D.C.: Institute for Palestine Studies, 1971.

Khalidi, Walid. "The Palestine Problem: An Overview." *Journal of Palestine Studies* 21, No. 1 (1991): 5-16. Http://www.palestine-studies.com/enakba/history/Khalidi,%20Walid_The%20Palestine%20Problem.pdf.

Kimmerling, Baruch. "Israel's Culture of Martyrdom." *The Nation*, January 10, 2005. http://www.thenation.com/article/israels-culture-martyrdom.

King, Henry C., and Charles R. Crane. *First Publication of King-Crane Report on the Near East; a Suppressed Official Document of the United States Government.* Report. 27th ed. Vol. 55. New York: Editor & Publisher, 1922. Online at http://wwi.lib.byu.edu/index.php/Introduction_of_the_Commission_Report.

Koestler, Arthur. *The Thirteenth Tribe: The Khazar Empire and Its Heritage.* New York: Random House, 1976.

Kolsky, Thomas A. *Jews against Zionism: The American Council for Judaism, 1942-1948.* Philadelphia: Temple UP, 1990.

Kurth, Peter. *American Cassandra: The Life of Dorothy Thompson.* Boston: Little, Brown, 1990.

Landman, Samuel. "Great Britain, the Jews and Palestine." *New Zionist*, 1936. http://desip.igc.org/1939sLandman.htm.

Langer, Felicia. *An Age of Stone.* London: Quartet Books, 1988.

Levinson, Jay. "House of HaRav Avraham Yitzchak Kook." *Jewish Mag*, March 2006. http://www.jewishmag.com/100mag/kook/kook.htm.

Lilienthal, Alfred M. *What Price Israel?* 50th Anniversary ed. Haverford, PA: Infinity Publishing, 2004.

Lilienthal, Alfred M. *The Zionist Connection: What Price Peace?* New York: Dodd, Mead, 1978.

Lippman, Thomas W. "The View from 1947: The CIA and the Partition of Palestine." *Middle East Journal* 61, no. 1 (2007): 17-28.

Maisel, Louis Sandy, Ira N. Forman, Donald Altschiller, and Charles Walker Bassett, Eds. *Jews in American Politics*. Lanham, MD: Rowman & Littlefield, 2004.

Malcolm, James A. *Origins of the Balfour Declaration: Dr. Weizmann's Contribution*. London: British Museum, 1944. Online at http://www.mailstar.net/malcolm.html.

Manuel, Frank E. "Judge Brandeis and the Framing of the Balfour Declaration." In *From Haven to Conquest: Readings in Zionism and the Palestine Problem until 1948*, 165-172. Washington, D.C.: Institute for Palestine Studies, 1987.

Martin, David. "Who Killed James Forrestal?" DC Dave. November 10, 2002. http://www.dcdave.com/article4/021110.html.

Marton, Kati. *A Death in Jerusalem*. New York: Arcade, 1996.

Masalha, Nur. *Expulsion of the Palestinians: The Concept of "Transfer" in Zionist Political Thought, 1882-1948*. 4th Ed. Washington, D.C.: Institute for Palestine Studies, 2001.

McCarthy, Justin. *The Population of Palestine: Population History and Statistics of the Late Ottoman Period and the Mandate*. New York: Columbia UP, 1990.

McGowan, Daniel A., and Marc H. Ellis. *Remembering Deir Yassin: The Future of Israel and Palestine*. New York: Olive Branch Press, 1998.

McGrory, Mary. "Return Engagement for Rabbi Korff." *St. Petersburg Times*, March 1, 1978. http://news.google.com/newspapers?nid=888&dat=19780301&id=oTYpAAAAIBAJ&sjid=s1kDAAAAIBAJ&pg=2729,94958.

Medoff, Rafael. "The Bergson Group vs. The Holocaust – and Jewish Leaders vs. Bergson." *The Jewish Press*, June 6, 2007. http://www.jewishpress.com/pageroute.do/21747.

Medoff, Rafael. *Militant Zionism in America: The Rise and Impact of the Jabotinsky Movement in the United States, 1926-1948*. Tuscaloosa: University of Alabama, 2002.

Menuhin, Moshe. *The Decadence of Judaism in Our Time*. Beirut: Institute for Palestine Studies, 1969.

Merkley, Paul Charles. *Christian Attitudes towards the State of Israel*. Montreal: McGill-Queen's University Press, 2001.

"MI5 Feared Zionist Air Raid Plan for London." *The Journal* (Northumberland), May 22, 2003. http://www.thefreelibrary.com/MI5+feared+Zionist+air+raid+plan+for+London.-a0102133325.

Morgenthau, Henry, and Peter Balakian. *Ambassador Morgenthau's Story*. Detroit: Wayne State University Press, 2003.

Morgenthau, Henry. *Mostly Morgenthaus: A Family History*. New York: Ticknor & Fields, 1991.

Excerpt: http://www.paulgassfamily.com/section3/iii3/iii3_003.htm#_ftnref5

Mulhall, John W., CSP. *America and the Founding of Israel: an Investigation of the Morality of America's Role.* Los Angeles: Deshon, 1995.

Murphy, Bruce Allen. *The Brandeis/Frankfurter Connection: The Secret Political Activities of Two Supreme Court Justices.* New York: Oxford UP, 1982.

Naeim, Gilad. "The Jews of Iraq." *The Link*, April/May 1998. http://www.ifamericansknew.org/history/ref-giladi.html.

Neff, Donald. *Fallen Pillars: U.S. Policy towards Palestine and Israel since 1945.* Reprint Ed. Washington D.C.: Institute for Palestine Studies, 2002.

Neff, Donald. *Fifty Years of Israel.* Washington, D.C.: American Educational Trust, 1998.

New York Times. "Judging Judges, and History." Editorial. February 18, 1982, Late City Final ed., Section A. http://www.nytimes.com/1982/02/18/opinion/judging-judges-and-history.html.

O Cathail, Maidhc. "Zionism's Un-Christian Bible." *Middle East Online*, November 2009, 25. http://www.middle-east-online.com/english/?id=35914.

O'Huallachain, D. L., and J. Forrest Sharpe, eds. *Neo-conned! Again: Hypocrisy, Lawlessness, and the Rape of Iraq.* Vienna, VA: Light in the Darkness Publications, 2005.

Orwell, George. *Nineteen Eighty-four.* New York: Harcourt, Brace, 1949.

Pace, Eric. "Baruch Korff, 81, Rabbi and Defender of Nixon." *New York Times*, July 27, 1995, Obituaries sec. http://www.nytimes.com/1995/07/27/obituaries/baruch-korff-81-rabbi-and-defender-of-nixon.html.

"The Palestine Mandate." The Avalon Project: Documents in Law, History, and Diplomacy. Accessed January 1, 2014.
http://avalon.law.yale.edu/20th_century/palmanda.asp.

Pappe, Ilan. *The Ethnic Cleansing of Palestine*. Oxford: Oneworld, 2007.

Patai, ed. *Encyclopaedia of Zionism and Israel*. Accessed January 1, 2014.
http://www.iahushua.com/Zion/zionhol10.html.

Perry, Mark. "Petraeus Wasn't the First." *Foreign Policy* (web log), April 1, 2010.
http://mideast.foreignpolicy.com/posts/2010/04/01/petraeus_wasnt_the_first.

"Peter Bergson." United States Holocaust Memorial Museum. June 10, 2013.
http://www.ushmm.org/wlc/en/article.php?ModuleId=10007041.

Philo, Greg, and Mike Berry. *More Bad News from Israel*. London: Pluto Press, 2011.

"Population Statistics: Israeli-Palestinian Conflict." ProCon.org. September 17, 2010.
http://israelipalestinian.procon.org/view.resource.php?resourceID=636.

"The Press: Free Speech for the Boss." *Time*, November 17, 1958.
http://www.time.com/time/magazine/article/0,9171,810661,00.html.

"Protestant Church Leader Warns Against Political Zionism; Says Judaism Is a Religion." *Jewish Telegraphic Agency* (New York), January 29, 1949.
http://archive.jta.org/article/1949/01/26/3017334/

protestant-church-leader-warns-against-political-zionism-says-judaism-is-a-religion.

"Question Authenticity Police Version of Plot." *Canadian Jewish Chronicle*, September 26, 1947. http://news.google.com/newspapers?nid=883&dat=19470926&id=jQFPAAAAIBAJ&sjid=jEwDAAAAIBAJ&pg=904,4915328.

Qumsiyeh, Mazin B. *Sharing the Land of Canaan: Human Rights and the Israeli-Palestinian Struggle*. London: Pluto Press, 2004.

Qumsiyeh, Mazin. "Palestinian Refugees Right to Return and Repatriation." In *Sharing the Land of Canaan: Human Rights and the Israeli-Palestinian Struggle*. London: Pluto, 2004. Online at http://ifamericansknew.org/history/ref-qumsiyeh.html.

"Rabbi Korff Announces Retirement from Nixon Fund." *Spartanburg Herald-Journal*, May 29, 1975. http://news.google.com/newspapers?nid=1876&dat=19750529&id=f5QeAAAAIBAJ&sjid=HcwEAAAAIBAJ&pg=7086,5202171.

Raider, Mark A. "'Irresponsible, Undisciplined Opposition': Ben Halpern on the Bergson Group and Jewish Terrorism in Pre-State Palestine." *American Jewish History* 92, no. 3 (2004): 313-60. http://muse.jhu.edu/journals/ajh/summary/v092/92.3raider.html.

Reinharz, Jehuda. "His Majesty's Zionist Emissary: Chaim Weizmann's Mission to Gibraltar in 1917." *Journal of Contemporary History* 27, no. 2 (1992): 259-77. http://www.jstor.org/stable/260910.

"Release of Rabbi Sought." *Advertiser* (Adelaide, SA), September 10, 1947. http://trove.nla.gov.au/ndp/del/article/35998232.

"Report - A Call to Courage: Reclaiming Our Liberties Ten Years After 9/11." *American Civil Liberties Union*, September 2011. https://www.aclu.org/files/assets/acalltocourage.pdf

Reynier, Jacques De. *1948 A□ Jerusalem*. Neucha□ tel: E□ ditions De La Baconnie□ re; (distribue□ Par Payot, Lausanne Et Paris), 1969.

Reynier, Jacques De. *A Jerusalem, Un Drapeau Flottait Sur La Ligne De Feu*. Neucha□ tel: Editions De La Baconie□ re, 1950.

Rich, Paul, ed. *Iraq and Gertrude Bell's The Arab of Mesopotamia*. Lanham, MD: Lexington Books, 2008.

Rosen, Robert N. *Saving the Jews: Franklin D. Roosevelt and the Holocaust*. New York: Thunder's Mouth Press, 2006. Online at http://books.google.com/books?id=mC1MFqELLpUC&dq=van+paassen+bergson+hoax&source=gbs_navlinks_s

Rosenberg, Rosalind. "Virginia Gildersleeve: Opening the Gates." *Living Legacies*, Summer 2001. http://www.columbia.edu/cu/alumni/Magazine/Summer2001/Gildersleeve.html.

Rubinstein, William D. *The Myth of Rescue: Why the Democracies Could Not Have Saved More Jews from the Nazis*. London: Routledge, 1997.

Rubinstein, William D. "The Secret of Leopold Amery." *History Today* 49 (February 1999). http://www.ifamericansknew.org/us_ints/amery.html.

Said, Edward W., and Christopher Hitchens. *Blaming the Victims: Spurious Scholarship and the Palestinian Question*. London: Verso, 1988.

Sand, Shlomo, and Yael Lotan. *The Invention of the Jewish People*. London: Verso, 2009.

Sanders, Marion K. *Dorothy Thompson: A Legend in Her Time*. New York: Avon Books, 1974.

Sanders, Ronald. *The High Walls of Jerusalem: A History of the Balfour Declaration and the Birth of the British Mandate for Palestine*. New York: Holt, Rinehart and Winston, 1984.

Sands of Sorrow. Produced by Council for the Relief of Palestine Arab Refugees. Narrated by Dorothy Thompson. 1950. http://www.youtube.com/watch?v=lQ6lIsl-pHU.

Sanua, Marianne Rachel. *Let Us Prove Strong: The American Jewish Committee, 1945-2006*. Waltham, MA: Brandeis UP, 2007.

Sarna, Jonathan D. *American Judaism: A History*. New Haven: Yale University Press, 2004.

Sarna, Jonathan D., Ellen Smith, and Scott-Martin Kosofsky, eds. *The Jews of Boston*. New Haven: Yale University Press, Combined Jewish Philanthropies of Greater Boston, 2005. Online at http://books.google.com/books/about/The_Jews_Of_Boston.html?id=sz5UJ1Lh21IC.

Saul, Norman E. *The Life and times of Charles R. Crane: 1858 - 1939; American Businessman, Philanthropist, and a Founder of Russian Studies in America*. Lanham, MD: Lexington Books, 2012.

Schmidt, Sarah. *Horace M. Kallen: Prophet of American Zionism*. Brooklyn, NY: Carlson, 1995.

Schmidt, Sarah. "The Parushim: A Secret Episode in American Zionist History." *American Jewish Historical Quarterly* 65, no. Dec (1975): 121-39.

"Securing the Dream." Jewish Historical Society of Greater Washington. Accessed January 1, 2014. http://www.jhsgw.org/exhibitions/online/jewishwashington/exhibition/securing-the-dream.

Segev, Tom. *The Seventh Million*. New York: Hill and Wang, 1993.

Shahak, Israel, and Norton Mezvinsky. *Jewish Fundamentalism in Israel*. London: Pluto Press, 1999.

Shahak, Israel. *Jewish History, Jewish Religion: the Weight of Three Thousand Years*. London: Pluto, 1997.

Sheean, Vincent. *Dorothy and Red*. Greenwich, CT: Fawcett Publications, 1964.

Sheean, Vincent. *Personal History*. Garden City, NY: Doubleday, Doran & Company, 1935.

Shlaim, Avi. *The Iron Wall: Israel and the Arab World*. New York: W.W. Norton, 2000.

Slater, Leonard. *The Pledge*. New York: Simon and Schuster, 1970.

Smith, Charles D. *Palestine and the Arab-Israeli Conflict*. New York: St. Martin's Press, 1996.

Smith, Grant F. *Declassified Deceptions: The Secret History of Isaiah L. Kenen and the Rise of the American Israel Public Affairs Committee (AIPAC)*. Washington, D.C.: Institute for Research: Middle Eastern Policy, 2007.

Smith, Grant F. *Spy Trade: How Israel's Lobby Undermines America's Economy*. Washington, D.C.: Institute for Research, Middle Eastern Policy, 2009.

Snetsinger, John. *Truman, the Jewish Vote, and the Creation of Israel*. Stanford, CA: Stanford University, 1974.

Sokolow, Nahum, and Arthur James Balfour. *History of Zionism (1600-1918), by Nahum Sokolow, with an*

Introduction by the Rt. Hon. A. J. Balfour,... Vol. 2.
London: Longmans, Green and, 1919.
https://archive.org/details/historyofzionism02sokou
oft.

Solomon, Norman, and Abba A. Solomon. "The Blind
Alley of J Street and Liberal American Zionism."
Huffington Post, January 22, 2014.
http://www.huffingtonpost.com/norman-
solomon/the-blind-alley-of-j-stre_b_4644658.html.

Stephens, Tom. "Civil Liberties After September
11." *CounterPunch*, July 11-13, 2003.
http://www.counterpunch.org/2003/07/11/civil-
liberties-after-september-11.

Stevens, Richard P. *American Zionism and U.S. Foreign Policy,
1942-1947*. Reprinted by the Institute for Palestine
Studies, 1970. New York: Pageant, 1962.

Stieglitz, Avi V. "Baruch Korff, 'Nixon's Rabbi' and
Activist, Dies of Cancer at 81." *Jweekly* (San
Francisco), August 4, 1995.
http://www.jweekly.com/article/full/1382/baruch-
korff-nixon-s-rabbi-and-activist-dies-of-cancer-at-
81/.

Strindberg, Anders. "Forgotten Christians." *The American
Conservative*, May 24, 2004.
http://www.amconmag.com/article/2004/may/24/0
0013/.

*Supplement to Survey of Palestine Notes Compiled for the
Information of the United Nations Special Committee on
Palestine*. Washington, D.C.: Institute for Palestine
Studies, 1991.

"Survivors' Accounts." Deir Yassin Remembered.
Accessed January 1, 2014.
http://www.deiryassin.org/survivors.html.

Tamari, Salim. *Jerusalem 1948: The Arab Neighbourhoods and Their Fate in the War.* Jerusalem: Institute of Jerusalem Studies: Center for Jerusalem Studies, 2002.

Thomson, Malcolm. "The Balfour Declaration: To the Editor of the Times." *The Times* (London), November 2, 1949, Letters sec.

"Ties That Bind: Washington Area Jews and the Birth of the State of Israel." Jewish Historical Society of Greater Washington. Accessed January 1, 2014. http://www.jhsgw.org/israel60/slideshow/secret-meetings.php.

"Time Line for Rabbi Avraham Yitzchak Kook (1865-1935)." RavKookTorah.org. Accessed January 1, 2014. http://www.ravkooktorah.org/timeline.htm.

"Timeline of Zionist Terror." Al-Nakba History. Accessed January 1, 2014. http://www.al-nakba-history.com/origins1948/unterrorismchronology.html.

Tivnan, Edward. *The Lobby: Jewish Political Power and American Foreign Policy.* New York: Simon and Schuster, 1987.

Tweedie, Neil, and Peter Day. "Jewish Groups Plotted to Kill Bevin." *Telegraph* (UK), May 22, 2003. http://www.telegraph.co.uk/news/1430766/Jewish-groups-plotted-to-kill-Bevin.html.

UK. The National Archives. *Possible Jewish Terrorist Attempts to Assassinate Ernest Bevin, Foreign Secretary.* 1945-1946. http://discovery.nationalarchives.gov.uk/SearchUI/details/C11602817?uri=C11602817-details. Reference: KV 2/3428

"UN Partition Plan." *BBC Online*, November 29, 2001. http://news.bbc.co.uk/2/hi/in_depth/middle_east/i

srael_and_the_palestinians/key_documents/1681322.
stm.

Uni, Assaf. "Hans Herzl's Wish Comes True - 76 Years
    Later." *Ha'aretz* (Tel Aviv), September 19, 2006.
    http://www.haaretz.com/print-edition/news/hans-
    herzl-s-wish-comes-true-76-years-later-1.197621.

United Nations. *Charter of the United Nations: Chapter I,
    Purposes and Principles.* Accessed January 1, 2014.
    http://www.un.org/en/documents/charter/chapter1
    .shtml.

"United Nations General Assembly Resolution 181." The
    Avalon Project: Documents in Law, History, and
    Diplomacy. Accessed January 1, 2014.
    http://www.yale.edu/lawweb/avalon/un/res181.htm

Urofsky, Melvin. *Louis D. Brandeis: A Life.* New York, NY:
    Pantheon Books, 2009.

Urofsky, Melvin. *We Are One: American Jewry and Israel.*
    Garden City, NY: Anchor Press/Doubleday, 1978.

"US Pilot Told Police of Bomb Plot, Was Asked to Raid
    London." *The Argus* (Melbourne), September 9, 1947.
    http://trove.nla.gov.au/ndp/del/article/22506150.

"U.S. War Ace Foiled Plot to Bomb London." *Herald
    Tribune* (New York), 1947.

Vanden Heuvel, William. "America, Franklin D. Roosevelt
    and the Holocaust." Address, Annual Franklin &
    Eleanor Roosevelt Distinguished Lecture, Roosevelt
    University, Chicago, IL, October 17, 1996.
    http://newdeal.feri.org/feri/wvh.htm.

Walton, Calder. "Excerpt: How Zionist Extremism
    Became British Spies' Biggest Enemy." *Foreign Policy,*
    January 2, 2014.
    http://www.foreignpolicy.com/articles/2014/01/01

/how_zionist_extremists_helped_create_britain_s_su
rveillance_state.

Weir, Alison. "Denying Nazi-Zionist Collusion: The
Sacramento Bee, Darrell Steinberg, and
Islamophobia." *CounterPunch*, March 4-6, 2011.
http://ifamericansknew.org/media/sacbee.html.

"Who Was Virginia Gildersleeve?" The Virginia
Gildersleeve International Fund. Accessed December
20, 2013. http://www.vgif.org/a_vg.shtml.

"Why Did Seven Well Equipped Arab Armies Attempt to
Destroy the Poorly Armed and Newly Founded
'Jewish State'?" Palestine Remembered. August 16,
2001.
http://www.palestineremembered.com/Acre/Palesti
ne-Remembered/Story457.html.

Wilson, Evan M. *Decision on Palestine: How the U.S. Came to
Recognize Israel.* Stanford, CA: Hoover Institution
Press, Stanford University, 1979.

Wilson, Evan M. *Jerusalem, Key to Peace.* Washington: Middle
East Institute, 1970.

"Woodrow Wilson." The White House. Accessed January
1, 2014.
http://www.whitehouse.gov/about/presidents/wood
rowwilson.

Woodward, Bob, and Carl Bernstein. *The Final Days.* New
York: Simon and Schuster, 1976.

Wright, Edwin M. *The Great Zionist Cover-up: A Study and
Interpretation.* Cleveland: Northeast Ohio Committee
on Middle East Understanding, 1975.

Wright, Edwin M. "Oral History Interview with Edwin M.
Wright." Interview by Richard D. McKinzie. Harry S.
Truman Library and Museum. August 1977.
http://www.trumanlibrary.org/oralhist/wright.htm.

Wyman, David S., and Hillel Kook. "The Bergson Group, America, and the Holocaust: A Previously Unpublished Interview with Hillel Kook/Peter Bergson." *American Jewish History* 89, no. 1 (2001): 3-34. http://muse.jhu.edu/journals/ajh/summary/v089/89.1wyman.html.

Yale, William. "Guide to the William Yale Papers, 1916-1972." MS MC 21, University of New Hampshire Library, Durham, NH. http://www.library.unh.edu/special/index.php/william-yale.

Yale, William. *The Near East: A Modern History.* Ann Arbor: University of Michigan Press, 1968.

"Yank Flyer Reveals Stern Gang Hired Him to Drop Bombs on British Foreign Office." *St. Petersburg Times,* September 10, 1947. http://news.google.com/newspapers?nid=888&dat=19470910&id=8VtIAAAAIBAJ&sjid=3E4DAAAAIBAJ&pg=2421,4272387.

"Zionists Plotted IRA-style Terrorism." *The Times* (London), May 22, 2003. http://www.thetimes.co.uk/tto/news/uk/article1908776.ece.

FURTHER READING

I read and cited a great many books and articles in writing this book, and numerous others that I will cite in part two. While all the books in my bibliography provided useful information, some I felt were flawed by the partisan nature of the author's predisposition and at times included statements that I felt were ill-supported by the facts.

Other books, however, I found particularly sound. While no book, including my own, can include all the facts on this fascinating history and none is perfect, I found the following books especially valuable sources of information on the regional and U.S. history during the time period addressed in my book, and I recommend them as a starting point for readers who wish to pursue this subject in greater depth. (The following list is in no way exhaustive, as I have limited myself to just ten listings in each category, causing me, reluctantly, to leave out many other equally superlative books.)

United States

Berger, Elmer. *Memoirs of an Anti-Zionist Jew*. Beirut: Institute for Palestine Studies, 1978.

Christison, Kathleen. *Perceptions of Palestine: Their Influence on U.S. Middle East Policy*. 1st ed. Berkeley, CA: University of California Press, 2000.

Green, Stephen. *Taking Sides, America's Secret Relations with a Militant Israel*. Brattleboro: Amana Books, 1988.

John, Robert and Hadawi, Sami. *The Palestine Diary.* New York: New World Press, 1970.

Hart, Alan. *Zionism: The Real Enemy of the Jews.* Atlanta, GA: Clarity Press, 2009.

Lilienthal, Alfred M. *What Price Israel?* 50th Anniversary ed. Haverford, PA: Infinity Publishing, 2004. *The Zionist Connection: What Price Peace?* New York: Dodd, Mead, 1978.

Mulhall, John W., CSP. *America and the Founding of Israel: an Investigation of the Morality of America's Role.* Los Angeles: Deshon, 1995.

Neff, Donald. *Fallen Pillars: U.S. Policy towards Palestine and Israel since 1945.* Reprint Ed. Washington D.C.: Institute for Palestine Studies, 2002.

Smith, Grant. *Declassified Deceptions: The Secret History of Isaiah L. Kenen and the Rise of the American Israel Public Affairs Committee (AIPAC).* Washington, D.C.: Institute for Research: Middle Eastern Policy, 2007. *Spy Trade: How Israel's Lobby Undermines America's Economy.* Washington, D.C.: Institute for Research, Middle Eastern Policy, 2009. Also, his numerous other books on this topic, see Institute for Research: Middle Eastern Policy: http://irmep.org/

Stevens, Richard P. *American Zionism and U.S. Foreign Policy, 1942-1947.* Reprinted by the Institute for Palestine Studies, 1970. New York: Pageant, 1962.

Middle East

Abu-Sitta, Salman H. *Atlas of Palestine, 1917-1966.* London: Palestine Land Society, 2010

Esber, Rosemarie M. *Under the Cover of War: The Zionist Expulsion of the Palestinians.* Alexandria, VA: Arabicus Books & Media, 2008.

Hadawi, Sami. *Bitter Harvest: Palestine Between 1914-1979*. New York: Caravan Books, 1979

Khalidi, Walid. *All That Remains: The Palestinian Villages Occupied and Depopulated by Israel in 1948*. Washington, D.C.: Institute for Palestine Studies, 1992.

Khalidi, Walid. *From Haven to Conquest: Readings in Zionism and the Palestine Problem until 1948*. Vol. 2. Washington, D.C.: Institute for Palestine Studies, 1971.

Masalha, Nur. *Expulsion of the Palestinians: The Concept of "Transfer" in Zionist Political Thought, 1882-1948*. 4th Ed. Washington, D.C.: Institute for Palestine Studies, 2001.

Pappé, Ilan. *The Ethnic Cleansing of Palestine*. Oxford: Oneworld, 2007.

Qumsiyeh, Mazin B. *Sharing the Land of Canaan: Human Rights and the Israeli-Palestinian Struggle*. London: Pluto Press, 2004.

Shlaim, Avi. *The Iron Wall: Israel and the Arab World*. New York: W.W. Norton, 2000.

Smith, Charles D. *Palestine and the Arab-Israeli Conflict:*. Boston, Mass.: Bedford/St. Martin's, 2013.

Other

Shahak, Israel, and Norton Mezvinsky. *Jewish Fundamentalism in Israel*. London: Pluto Press, 1999.

Shahak, Israel. *Jewish History, Jewish Religion: the Weight of Three Thousand Years*. London: Pluto, 1997.

INDEX

C

L

M

N

In 2000, ALISON WEIR left her home in California to travel alone to Palestine and Israel as an independent journalist, to see the Middle East conflict first-hand. What she uncovered led her to feel this was one of the most significant and least understood issues for Americans today. Now Executive Director of If Americans Knew and President of the Council for the National Interest, Weir tirelessly studies the conflict, its history, and the US connection and travels the world speaking of her experiences and research.

CPSIA information can be obtained at www.ICGtesting.com
Printed in the USA
LVOW05s2307021014

407081LV00013B/166/P